LAYOUT
AND GRAPHIC DESIGN

195AC

D0464448

LAYOUT
AND GRAPHIC DESIGN

RAYMOND A. BALLINGER

 **VAN NOSTRAND REINHOLD COMPANY** New York

STUDIO VISTA London

225355

Z
253.5
B28
1970

TO EDWARD WARWICK

ARTIST, EDUCATOR AND FRIEND

AND

TO CHARLES T. COINER

ARTIST, DESIGNER, ART DIRECTOR;

SPONSOR OF SOME OF AMERICA'S

GREAT PAGE DESIGNS

Copyright © 1970 by Reinhold Book Corporation.

Library of Congress Catalog Card No. 72-90309.
British SBN 289 79634 2.

All rights reserved. No part of this work covered by the copyright hereon may be reproduced or used in any form or by
any means—graphic, electronic, or mechanical, including
photocopying, recording, taping, or information storage and
retrieval systems—without written permission of the publisher.
Manufactured in the United States of America.

Published in the United States of America by Van Nostrand
Reinhold Company, 450 West 33rd Street, New York, N.Y. 10001,
and in Great Britain by Studio Vista Ltd., Blue Star House,
Highgate Hill, London N19.

Published simultaneously in Canada by D. Van Nostrand
Company (Canada), Ltd.

Designed by Raymond A. Ballinger.
Printed by Halliday Lithograph Corporation.
Bound by William Marley Company.

1 3 5 7 9 11 13 15 16 14 12 10 8 6 4 2

N.J.S.U. LIBRARY
FARGO, N.D.

CONTENTS

Note: The four-color reproduction process is demonstrated on the fold-out jacket.

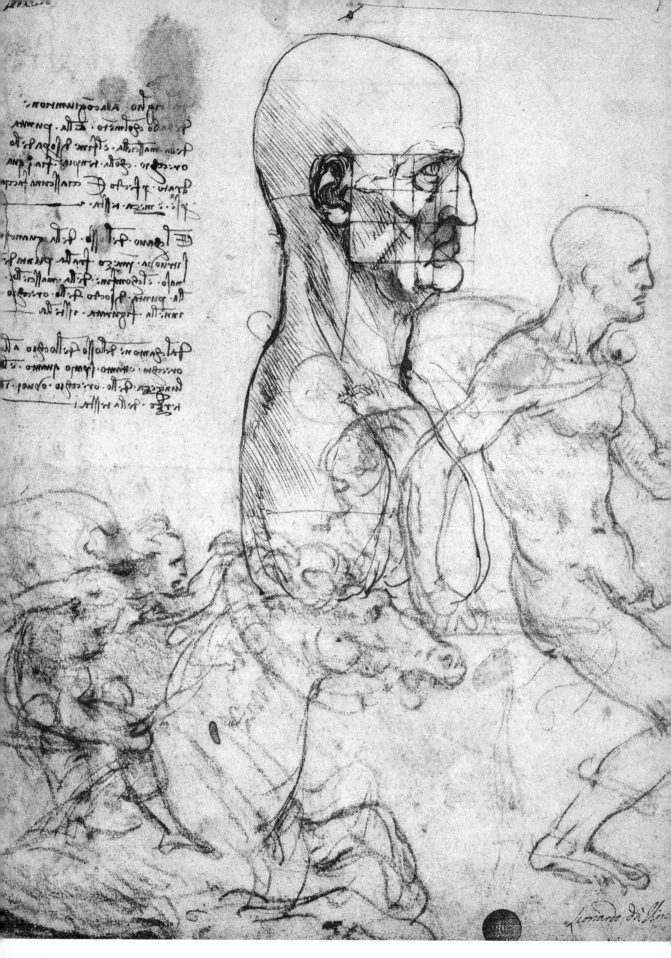

Preliminary rough for a layout by the author

This book begins, fittingly enough, with the two reproductions on these pages, both of which are done in the spirit of free sketching which is the basis of all good design and page layout. Because the book is planned essentially for students of the graphic arts I would like here to express my gratitude for the privilege of having taught and worked with many students who have stimulated me in my work and who have gone on to success in their own right. At the same time I wish to express my appreciation to all who have permitted reproduction of their works, many of which were shown in my earlier book titled *Layout*. I would like to include a special note of appreciation to Mr. Robert Bach, Mr. Phil Eitzen and Mr. Robert Dunning of N. W. Ayer & Son, Inc., for the help they gave to me in the preparation of the work presented on pages 70 through 75. The constant enthusiasm of my editor, Mr. Jean Koefoed, for a revised edition of *Layout* prepared especially for students has stimulated me to produce the present work, which I hope will be, in turn, encouraging and instructive.

R. A. B.

FOREWORD

Whenever an artist applies his talents to the preparation of a piece of art he is at once facing the interesting problem of composition. When composition is applied to the format of a page it is known as layout, the subject of this book.

Surprisingly there are few books which deal specifically with this important application of art. This book has been planned to give the student who is interested in the graphic arts a foundation of knowledge and as much inspiration as possible about layout. In addition, *Layout and Graphic Design* can be used as a teaching text. In each section of the book I have presented projects in various aspects of layout, which may easily be used as assignments. Layout is a combination of talent, creative activity and general knowledge, and the project suggestions are intended to encourage the student to bring all these elements to bear and to create his own examples of successful theory and practice.

I hope that the student artist who plans to become involved in the creation of beautiful printed pages — layouts — will have had a basic training in art and some experience in using the tools and materials of the artist (plus a good general educational background). This will enable him to approach the subject in an exciting and original way.

In selecting illustrations of examples of good layouts for this book, I have deliberately used some material of an older vintage, simply because I believe that students in any subject should be aware of the fine things of the past as well as of contemporary successes — of which many examples are also included. It is for the student generation of today to evolve the useful and beautiful pages which will be left as the heritage of our time.

It's a new <u>kind</u>
of low-priced car!

The 1953 PLYMOUTH
will arrive at your Plymouth
dealer's Thursday,
November 20th

client   PLYMOUTH
agency   N. W. AYER & SON, INC.
art director   CALVIN ANDERSON
artist   CALVIN ANDERSON

BEGIN WITH DOODLES

Doodling is fun! For our purposes, we can forgo any discussion of whether the doodle is a bona fide art form. It is unquestionably an interesting approach to the exploration of page design. The splashy forms shown here were done by a large brush with great spontaneity and zest. They create an interesting composition and suggest the manner in which many actual examples of layouts have been developed. The text you are reading here and the illustration, placed with the doodle, make this page in itself a layout.

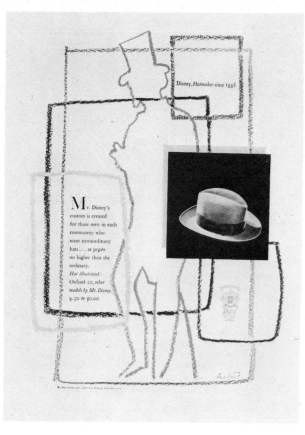

client DISNEY, INC.
agency WILLIAM WEINTRAUB & COMPANY, INC.
art director PAUL RAND
artist PAUL RAND

publication HARPER'S BAZAAR
art director ALEXEY BRODOVITCH
artist LUCHA TRUEL

client CONTAINER CORPORATION OF AMERICA
agency N. W. AYER & SON, INC.
art directors WALTER REINSEL, NEIL FUJITA
artist RAYMOND A. BALLINGER

In developing a page design for the Container Corporation of America the author used a doodle approach to the project. Many sketches were developed. One of the preliminary roughs is shown here together with the page which was accepted and printed.

PROJECT ASSIGNMENT: For experimenting with doodle compositions, use pads of artist's tissue paper (not ordinary tissue paper) or bond paper or sheets of inexpensive one- or two-ply Bristol board. It will help to cut the paper or board to a size similar to that of the pages of many popular weekly and monthly magazines — about 10$\frac{1}{2}$″ x 13″. Begin with a large watercolor brush and black ink or black poster paint. With the brush and the chosen medium, apply doodles to the page, working freely and with zest. Seek interesting forms and shapes and try to create appealing compositions. After you have completed some compositions in black and white, extend the scope of the project by using a second color medium (color ink, poster color, or dye) in conjunction with the black. This does not mean that the black and the color will be mixed; they should be treated as separate but related color forms, in the manner of the design shown on page 9. The two-color page happens to be an economical and popular type of layout.

ABOUT COLLAGE

Collage has a long history as an artistic technique — it has been used by Georges Braque, Pablo Picasso, and many other artists. The word "collage" is of French derivation and means literally "pasting." By extension it means an artistic composition of fragments pasted on a surface. In preparing collages artists often use a variety of materials (some of which they may prepare themselves) which they cut and tear, then arrange and paste into desired compositions. This is as much fun as doodling, and is also a very good takeoff point for experimentation. Doodling and collage can often work happily in combination with each other. In its truest sense, collage is not intended to be realistic — it presents the opportunity to experiment with and to distort the factual, and this creates much of its charm and interest. The collage below was made by the author from scraps and fragments in his studio.

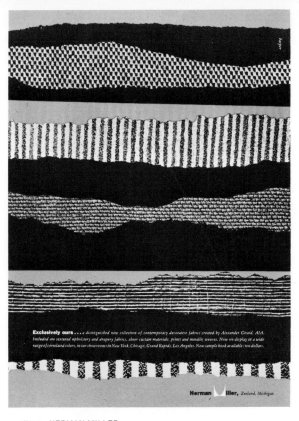

client HERMAN MILLER
agency GEORGE NELSON AND ASSOCIATES
designer IRVING HARPER
GEORGE NELSON AND ASSOCIATES

client RADIOTELEVISIONE ITALIANA
designer ERBERTO CARBONI

client CAMDEN COURIER-POST
agency RINGOLD/KALISH & CO.
art director BURT GREENSPAN
designer LEONARD WEXLER
artist LEONARD WEXLER
copywriter HOWARD RICE

client COLLINS, MILLER & HUTCHINGS, INC.
designer FRED HAUCK OF BEALL-HAUCK

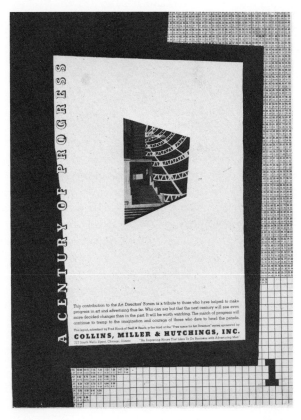

client MAISON DE LA PENSÉE FRANÇAISE
artist HENRI MATISSE

PROJECT ASSIGNMENT: In experimenting with collage, let the imagination run free without inhibitions. Cut an inexpensive mount board to a size to encourage freedom of approach — about 14″ x 18″. Use the vertical or the horizontal dimension. Sheets of gray packing board or corrugated board make interesting backgrounds. You can use the natural color or paint them with a base color of poster paint. Cut and mount any materials that strike your fancy, such as construction papers, textured papers, fabrics, plastics, wood. Paste these to the background in interesting compositions, seeking to create relationships of size, color, and texture that are appealing. Do not be concerned with making a picture of something. You may, however, after several experiments, want to try some "abstractions" of related objects. Collages made by cutting sections of pictures from magazines can be most interesting and may even be good enough to be used to decorate your classroom, studio or home.

GEOMETRIC AND OTHER FORMS

Nothing could be more unlike the doodle than the geometric form. The moment any form is applied to paper, a layout begins. The triangle, the square, the circle, the oval can be the basis of interesting compositions. It is probable that only a computer could calculate the number of positions in which, let us say, a triangle can be placed on a page, and each placement creates, of course, a new composition. When we experiment with the kinds, sizes and colors of triangles we begin to feel a real surge and interest in creating. So it is with other geometric forms. We may begin to explore the uses of more complicated forms such as the star, the arrow and the asterisk and other punctuation marks. Some very intriguing layouts using geometric forms and other more specific simple shapes are shown here in actual applications. Forms such as these are particularly adaptable to the design of posters.

client   FRETZ BROTHERS, LTD.
designer STAFF ARTISTS

client   THE DRAKE PRESS
publication THE NEW DRAKE IMPRESSIONS
art directors WILLIAM A. HIRSCH, JOSEPH GERING
artist   JOSEPH GERING

PROJECT ASSIGNMENT: For this project, use a white Bristol or illustration board cut to about 10$\frac{1}{2}$″ x 13″. Using your ingenuity and imagination as to size and placement, apply black triangles to the white background. You may be surprised to find that it takes considerable ability to cut or draw a neat triangle! A T-square, angles, pencils, a ruling pen, brushes, and black ink or poster paint will be needed if you plan to draw the triangles; black paper and a cutting blade will be sufficient if you plan to paste them. Experiment with different sizes and proportions of triangles, but solve the design in the geometric spirit of the triangular forms. Later experiments should include the addition of other geometric forms — circles, squares, and ovals, hexagons, stars, etc. Any of these will certainly test your design abilities. Extend the project, too, by the use of additional colors with the black. Projects using simple symbolic forms such as asterisks and other punctuation marks, hearts and arrows can be a further step toward background sources for composition — and layout.

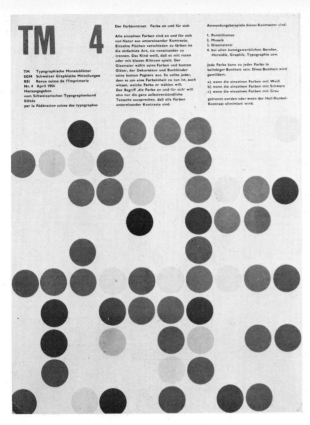

publication   TM TYPOGRAPHISCHE MONATSBLÄTTER
artist   EMIL RUDER

publication   IDEA, NO. 4, 1954, TOKYO, JAPAN
client   NIPPON BEER CO., LTD.
art director   HIDEO MUKAI
artist   YUSAKU KAMEKURA

client   OLIVETTI CORPORATION OF AMERICA
agency   THE CAPLES COMPANY
art director   LEO LIONNI
artist   LEO LIONNI

These examples of professional layouts exhibit the use of simple geometric forms such as triangles and circles. Note how similar forms have been used in more complicated arrangements involving other elements.

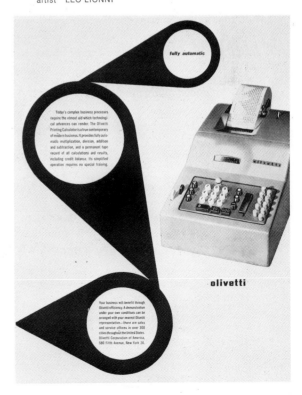

LETTER AND TYPE FORMS

Letter and type forms are basic design elements in layout; we come in contact with them every day. On pages 61 through 69 you will find some specific information about type and typography. At this point it seems sufficient merely to suggest that letter and type forms may be the inspiration for exciting compositions and layouts in which these forms are used alone or in a composition with other materials. Experiments can start with many different kinds of letters and type: your own doodle type of lettering, type from typographer's fonts, old wood types, stencils, the recently developed letter and type forms available on acetate, cutouts from magazines, etc. Some interesting possibilities are suggested on the page to the left. In the composition below, designer Walter Stait has made an interesting arrangement of type material, while a distinguished manufacturer of transfer type materials uses a display composed of parts of letter forms. The layout artist often finds his work involved in the areas of three dimensions, such as display.

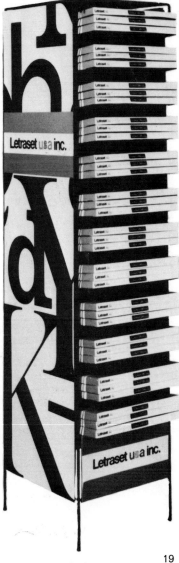

WALTER STAIT

client   LETRASET U.S.A. INC.
designers ASSOCIATED TECHDATA AND
          BLACK & MUSEN, INC.

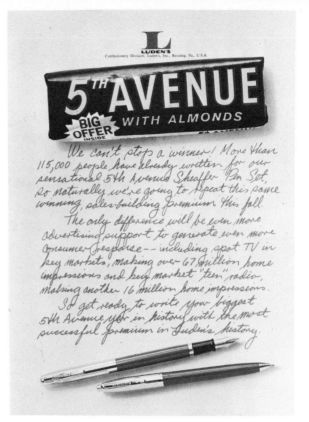

client ACI FILMS, INC.
publication REDISCOVERY-ART MEDIA
art director GEORGE KOIZUMI
artist GEORGE KOIZUMI

client LUDEN'S INC.
agency PHILA. AGENCY
art director HERMAN VOLZ
designer MARCENE GOODMAN
photographer TOM MEEHAN

PROJECT ASSIGNMENT: There can be numerous approaches to design projects using letters of one kind or another. For one approach, cut letters and type from old magazines; position and paste them experimentally (collage fashion) to create interesting compositions. For a second approach, use marking pens or pencils, writing informally and creating interesting compositions as you proceed (note the layout above in which simple handwriting has been used effectively). If you are fortunate enough to have access to the materials in a typesetting shop, try setting the text of a poem, a well-known nursery rhyme, or a famous statement in an unusual, expressive design suggestive of the text material. Older printing shops often have old wood type. It is interesting in itself (and getting scarce) and encourages experimental expression. Stencils and other equipment from a sign shop or stationery store offer ideas to the imaginative designer. Express yourself with type or letters on page sizes similar to the actual printed page sizes suggested previously — about 10$\frac{1}{2}$" x 13".

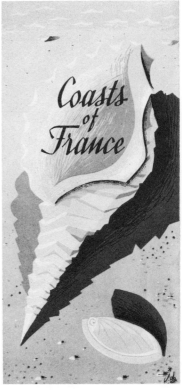

client   FRENCH GOVT. TOURIST OFFICE
artist   V. DIZAMBOURG

PICTORIAL RESOURCES

The concepts presented thus far in this book may be considered sound basics for good design and composition. A logical next step in exploring the theories of layout is the use of simple objects as pictorial elements on a page. It must be understood that the ultimate purpose of layout is to communicate as fully as possible with the beholder. While doodles, collage, geometric forms and letters, with which we have dealt thus far, can be attractive and interesting, there is no doubt that the observer of a page is more interested in seeing "things," particularly things with which he is familiar, such as seashells, keys, tools, utensils and other everyday, commonplace objects which he enjoys and uses or may desire to possess. Drawing and designing these objects extends the challenge to design ability and also, as a visual device, extends the purposes of the page.

C A R O N

LES POUDRES DE RIZ LES PLUS FINES
LES PARFUMS LES PLUS DELICATS

client   PARFUMS CARON
agency   ALBERT FRANK–GUENTHER LAW, INC.
artist   DRAWING BY PARFUMS CARON, PARIS, FRANCE

PROJECT ASSIGNMENT: You will have a great deal of respect for the rendering of seemingly simple objects after you have made some attempts of your own to extract their design beauty. You are ready to try this now. For this project look around your studio or home and select some simple item. First, make a drawing in silhouette of the object, trying to simplify it in the most elegant way you can in the manner of the items shown on the page to the right. Do this with several objects, using, in all cases, black ink or black poster paint. Then, as a second approach, draw these or other objects in direct, simple line in the manner of this handsome page for Caron. For a third approach, render some simple objects in dimension, decoratively, using gray values, as has been done in the design of the seashell on page 21. In this project do not bother with total page layout but concentrate on making the finest simplified drawings you can of the objects you have chosen.

SURFACE PREPARATION

client E. I. DU PONT DE NEMOURS & CO. (INC.)
studio TALONE & LA BRASCA, INC.
art director LARRY SCHAFLE
designer LARRY SCHAFLE
artists ED HARTMANN/LARRY SCHAFLE
copywriter LARRY PEARSON

GENERAL

Proper surface preparation is essential to obtain maximum protection at minimum cost. Du Pont plants have adopted the following standards with outstanding results.

Before applying any coat, whether prime, intermediate, or top coat, remove all contamination and loose material, i.e., chemicals, dirt, dust, oil, grease, extruded sap, pitch, loose paint, loose rust, loose mill scale and calcimine.

The characteristics of the coating, the service or atmosphere to which it is exposed, economics and location of the job, are the main factors that determine the actual method of surface preparation.

In general, no surface shall be prepared that is not to be primed the same day. This is mandatory for metal surfaces or where overnight contamination is likely to occur.

Listed below are surface conditions with appropriate cleaning methods and tools. The method selected must take into account surrounding conditions, including operating personnel and equipment.

Dirt and Dust—remove by vacuum brushing, or by washing with detergent and water. If surface is washed, it should be thoroughly dried before applying any coating.

Water Soluble Chemical Contamination—remove by washing with clean water.

Oil, Grease and Solvent-Soluble Chemical Contamination—remove by a solvent wash or by steam-cleaning guns using cleaning agents such as trisodium phosphate, or caustic, followed by flushing with clean water. Typical solvents for removing oil and grease are Triclene', Perclene', naphtha, mineral spirits, turpentine, or Du Pont No. 200T Dulux' Thinner. The solvent used should be free of oil or grease and the cloths should be changed frequently to prevent spreading oil by local supervision for safety.

Paint (loose or deteriorated)—remove by blasting, blowtorch, paint remover, paint scrapers, abrasive papers, or hand or power chisels or choppers. Cement- or lime-base water paints should be removed by scraping, wire brushing, or with live steam. Steam-cleaning guns, with chemical cleaners, may also be used.

Gloss of Paint—remove with sandpaper, steel wool, or solvent wash.

Mildew—remove by scraping followed by washing thoroughly with a solution of trisodium phosphate (1'. ounces to a gallon of water) and a clear water rinse.

Moisture and Dirt—remove from all cracks, crevices, and entire surface with compressed air or vacuum, before applying primer and each succeeding coat of the system.

Wax—remove by an approved solvent. See Oil, Grease and Solvent-Soluble Chemical Contamination.

company THOMAS C. THOMPSON COMPANY
publication CATALOG OF ENAMELS & SUPPLIES
art director DON DAHMS, THE BROWER COMPANY
designer HERB JONES & ASSOCIATES

publisher ART EDUCATION, INC.
publication ART: OF WONDER & A WORLD
art director NORMAN LALIBERTÉ
designer NORMAN LALIBERTÉ

Olives from Spain

FROM Seville, in sunny Spain, where climate and soil combine to make the finest olive growing district in the world come Heinz Queen Olives. The same region produces ripe olives for olive oil. And in the midst of these olive groves there is a Heinz establishment where the fruit is prepared under our strict supervision and the ripe olives are pressed for Heinz Imported Olive Oil.

Olives and raisins from Spain, currants from Greece, figs from Turkey, spices from Java and India, fruits and vegetables from the garden spots of America! The whole world is drawn on for the products used in making the 57 Varieties. And wherever quick handling is necessary to preserve freshness, Heinz kitchens are located right on the spot.

All these world-wide activities are for the purpose of making each food that bears the name Heinz pure and wholesome and good to eat—uniform in quality, and sufficient in quantity to supply a world-wide demand for them.

H. J. HEINZ COMPANY
57 Varieties

client H. J. HEINZ COMPANY
agency CALKINS & HOLDEN
artist EDWARD PENFIELD

client   JAS. HENNESSY & CO.
artist   E. R. COUSE

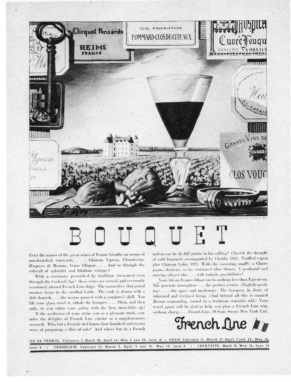

client   FRENCH LINE
agency   N. W. AYER & SON, INC.
art director   LEON KARP
artist   PIERRE ROY

THE ILLUSTRATION IN LAYOUT

For the communication in a layout to be best served by a total pictorial concept, some type of illustration is required. In today's graphic art world the term "illustration" includes anything of a complete pictorial nature — illustration, fashion illustration, product illustration, humorous illustration. An illustration, therefore, is any piece of art or photography which pictorializes a complete idea. In an editorial page it may be used to enhance a story or to show ideas about fashion, decoration, foods, sports and other areas of human activity. In an advertising page it may be used to create an appropriate and appealing atmosphere or to show the product itself. Since illustration is a highly specialized talent, the illustrator or photographer often works with the layout artist or art director in preparing layout pages.

client   PHILA. EVENING BULLETIN
agency   N. W. AYER & SON, INC.
art director   CHARLES HAYDEN
designer   CHARLES HAYDEN
artist   BOB MILNAZIK

PROJECT ASSIGNMENT: Since you may feel that you are not advanced enough in your art background to tackle actual illustrations, this project can be developed with illustrations or photographs cut from old magazines and arranged in your own experimental way on page layouts. For the text you can either cut type from magazines and paste it in the desired position, or use the ruled-line technique (see pages 31 and 65). On the other hand, you may want to experiment with your own sketch illustrations, exactly as a layout artist does professionally. Make a study of the different approaches to editorial pages as compared to advertising pages in the magazines and then decide which kind to do for your experiments — or do both! A page size of about 11″ x 13½″ would be good to start. Note that many editorial pages are double-page spreads — use this, too, as a challenging change from the single-page shape.

HUMOR IN LAYOUT

Though the idea to be presented may be entirely serious, humorous or cartoon illustration may often be used to gain attention and interest. It takes a very talented and unusual artist or photographer to create humorous material that is artistic, tasteful and truly *humorous.* It also takes a good sense of layout design to relate these pieces to a layout page, just as it does with a serious illustration or photograph. Note that one of the examples below is a poster using a delightful humorous figure. A poster is essentially a layout, but it is often prepared for a jumbo size. A good designer realizes, however, that a poster is intended to draw the attention of a beholder who is generally in motion and probably at a distance and its message must, therefore, be simple, direct, bold, dramatic. As for humor itself, the three examples shown here should indicate that it can be communicated in very different styles, depending on the nature of the project at hand.

client CHAS. PFIZER & CO., INC.
publication PFIZER SPECTRUM
art director ERLE YAHN
artist ERLE YAHN

client BATA
artist HERBERT LEUPIN

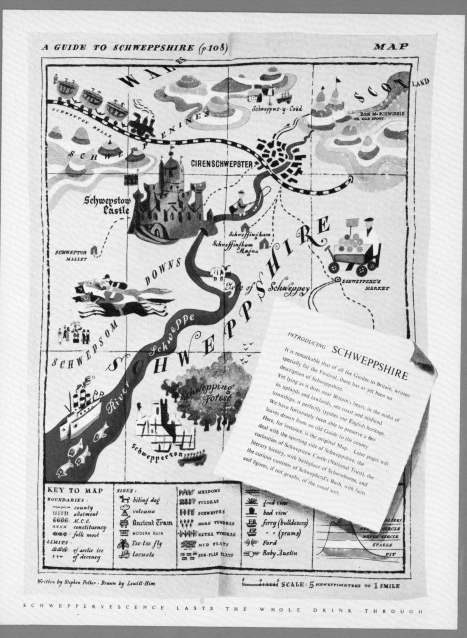

client SCHWEPPES, LTD.
art director F. C. HOOPER
artists LEWITT-HIM

PROJECT ASSIGNMENT: You may have thought of pictorial humor as restricted to the cartoon. The three examples shown here should broaden your perception and stimulate you to try some experimental humorous layouts. One suggestion is to try a double-spread editorial layout involving the characteristics of some political figure or figures; these might be done in black-and-white line with brush or pen or they might be concocted from pasteups of clipped sections of magazine photographs. After reviewing the following section on photography (and assuming that you use a camera) you can deliberately go out to seek humorous situations to use in layouts. Or, taking a hint from the reproductions above, you can do a humorous map for some imaginative subject in your own style. You will probably be surprised at what fun you have — and can make.

publication HOUSE & GARDEN
art editor WOLFGANG FYLER
art director ALEXANDER LIEBERMAN
photographer IRVING PENN

client PARFUMS CARON
agency ALBERT FRANK–GUENTHER LAW, INC.
photographer PARFUMS CARON, PARIS, FRANCE

THE CAMERA

Before the advent of the camera the job of illustrating ideas and objects always fell to the pencil, pen and brush. In today's design world the camera is an important tool of communication. Many of today's outstanding photographers have been trained as artists and have turned to the camera as their means of artistic expression. The layout artist or art director planning a page often has to make the basic decision of whether to employ illustrations or photography, and he also has to decide the spirit of the approach — illustrative, decorative, humorous, etc. If he takes the option of a photographic approach he will find that here, too, talent is essential, for an uninteresting photograph is no more useful than an uninspired illustration or a humorless cartoon. Even in the planning stages of a layout the camera has come to be a helpful sketching tool for ideas; this use of the camera is discussed on pages 58 and 59.

Suntones

This is **Sun Blond**, fairest of all the skin-blended Cosmetone nylons. Dip your legs in the magic of Phoenix sunlight colors, dull-pigmented and high-twist to make the legs appear smaller. As you tan change to a deeper shade. Suntones come in three intensities.

Phoenix | HIGH TWIST / CUSTOM-FIT / PROPORTIONS

client PHOENIX HOSIERY COMPANY
agency HOCKADAY ASSOCIATES
art director ALVIN CHERESKIN
photographer HERBERT MATTER

PROJECT ASSIGNMENT: Most people who have an interest in art have some experience with a camera, and if you are one of these people, you are already prepared to make some experiments with your own photographic layouts. Probably your stockpile of interesting negatives will furnish you with subject matter to begin. Think first in terms of unusual treatments of your prints, such as intelligent cropping (which all good layout artists are adept at doing) or silhouetting the important subject matter. Use such basic techniques as photographs made by placing actual objects directly on sensitized paper (in a darkroom, of course), exposing to light, and developing the print in the usual manner. If you have never experimented with photography, turn to your old magazines again and clip photographs. If you happen to own a Polaroid Land camera, read the material on page 58 and then devise some interesting projects for yourself.

ELEMENTS IN A LAYOUT

When we begin to consider the structure of a layout, it is appropriate to learn what the various elements that make up a layout are and what the proper terminology for them is. The individual elements listed here may be found in many layouts, although any given layout may not contain all of them.

HEADING. The line, usually in heavier type, set above the text or body matter. Also called a head or headline.

SUBHEAD. Secondary material set in smaller type, usually under the heading.

ILLUSTRATION. This may be any type of illustrative material — realistic, decorative, or humorous; painted, drawn, or photographed; black and white, color, or both.

SECONDARY ILLUSTRATION. The term applied to smaller or supplementary pictorial material.

PICTURE CAPTION. Small type material under, over or beside illustrations or secondary illustrations explaining the pictures.

TEXT. The type material containing the main message of the page.

LOGO. The design or symbol of an organization, used on many advertising pages. Also called a logotype or trademark.

SIGNATURE. The name of an organization or advertiser, usually set in type but often in a style peculiar to the individual organization or related to the logo.

The two diagrams of layouts below show all of these elements, first in a symmetrical format and then in an asymmetrical format. The requirements of any given project will determine which of the elements will be required and which will not. It should be noted, too, that the elements very often do not appear in the order listed here.

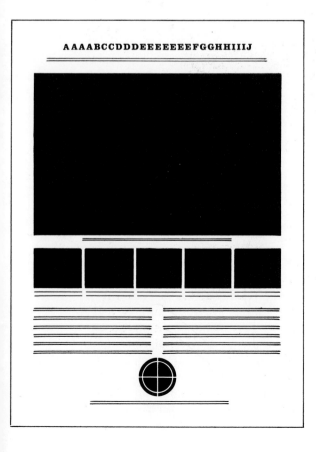
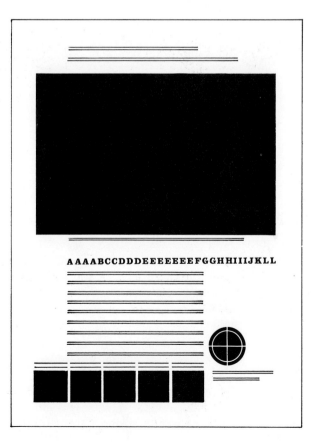

LAYOUT STRUCTURE ONE — SYMMETRY

"Rules" for design and composition are difficult to establish and are apt to become restrictive. Broadly speaking, layout and composition are expressions of balance, proportion and spatial relations to which have been added the ingenuity and taste of the designer. Nevertheless, some basic principles may help in the layout of the page. For example, let us consider a page which is intended to communicate a great sense of stability, sincerity and trustworthiness. A symmetrical, or *coaxial*, design may be used to help suggest these qualities. The design of this page, illustrating the theory, is built on the coaxial plan, with the symmetrical design of the old print placed under the equally symmetrical mechanical symbol. The famous designer A. M. Cassandre created the excellent poster on the opposite page in type in a symmetrical structure.

6 OCTOBRE - 6 NOVEMBRE 1950
MUSÉE
DES ARTS DÉCORATIFS
PALAIS DU LOUVRE
PAVILLON DE MARSAN
107 RUE DE RIVOLI
EXPOSITION

de 1925

A. M. CASSANDRE

À 1950

THÉATRE
AFFICHES
ARTS GRAPHIQUES
PEINTURE DÉCORATIVE
TOUS LES JOURS
SAUF LE MARDI
DE 10ʰ A 12ʰ ET DE 14ʰ A 17ʰ
PRIX D'ENTRÉE 80 FRS

AFFICHE D'INTERIEUR

client   MUSÉE DES ARTS DÉCORATIFS
artist   A. M. CASSANDRE

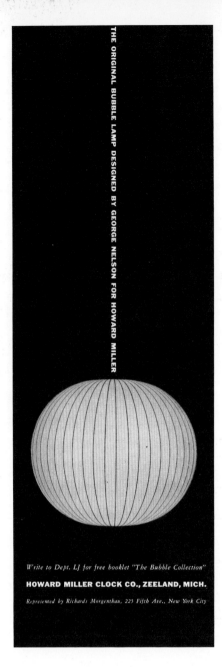

THE ORIGINAL BUBBLE LAMP DESIGNED BY GEORGE NELSON FOR HOWARD MILLER

Write to Dept. LJ for free booklet "The Bubble Collection"

HOWARD MILLER CLOCK CO., ZEELAND, MICH.

Represented by Richards Morgenthau, 225 Fifth Ave., New York City

client HOWARD MILLER CLOCK CO.
agency GEORGE NELSON AND ASSOCIATES
artist TOBIAS O'MARA
GEORGE NELSON AND ASSOCIATES

PROJECT ASSIGNMENT: Lay out some strictly symmetrical pages. Now that you are familiar with some of the basic techniques of layout design, put them to use — collage, type or letters, pictures, geometric forms. Or, as is often necessary, use two or three of these techniques to create pages all based on symmetry. Keep testing the axial balances of your pages so that you will have a clear concept of this type of page structure. For added interest add two or more colors to your compositions.

LAYOUT STRUCTURE TWO — ASYMMETRY

The asymmetrical approach to page structure is more subtle than the symmetrical approach — and quite informal. It has a freedom and exuberance quite unlike the symmetrical page. However, it requires its own discipline: a keen sense of balance and rhythm, of proportion and weight. The asymmetrical page may be likened to a dancer whose body moves at times slowly and at times swiftly, from position to position, yet ever with perfect balance, rhythm and grace. In contemporary graphic arts the asymmetrical page is very common. However, there are many superb asymmetrical pages of other eras. The author has deliberately designed this page in asymmetrical composition, offsetting the beautiful photograph of the dancer with the diagrammatic line drawings. It will be noted that the type, too, is placed somewhat differently than on most pages of the book.

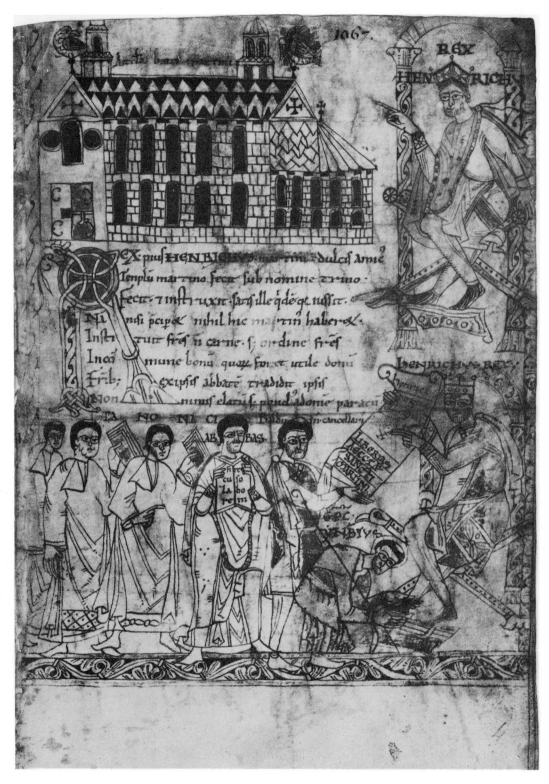

BRITISH MUSEUM—CHRONICLE OF THE ABBEY OF ST. MARTIN DES CHAMPS, PARIS, 11TH CENTURY

client   JOYCE, INC.
agency   N. W. AYER & SON, INC.
director   LEO LIONNI
artist   ARTHUR WILLIAMS

client   CHIPMAN KNITTING MILLS
agency   BOZELL & JACOBS
art director HOWARD RICHMAN
photographer JOHN STEWART

client   THE TRAVELERS INSURANCE COMPANY
agency   YOUNG & RUBICAM, INC.
art director HARLOW ROCKWELL
artist   KEN THOMPSON

client   KAISER-WILLYS
agency   WILLIAM H. WEINTRAUB & COMPANY, INC.
art director MILTON ACKOFF
photographer NEW CENTER STUDIOS

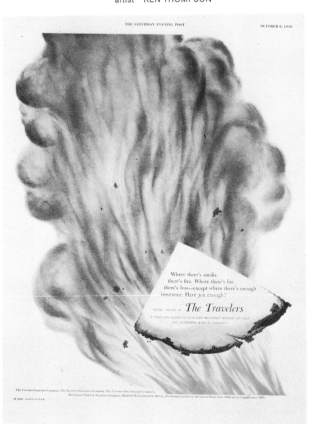

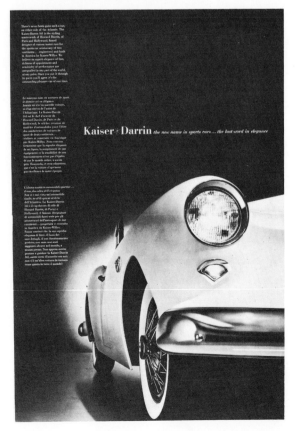

publication   TYPOGRAPHIE
publisher   ARTHUR NIGGLI LTD.
designer   EMIL RUDER

PROJECT ASSIGNMENT: Probably you fell quite naturally into the informal spirit of asymmetry in preparing page designs using doodles, collages or geometric forms in projects proposed earlier in this book. At this point it might be interesting to review the designs to see whether you feel that they have a good sense of organization and informal balance. Then you can design some pages in asymmetrical organization, making an effort to compose real layouts that include elements that you usually see on a page — heading, text, logo, etc. Make this project more interesting and realistic by deliberately choosing a product or service around which to plan your pages, or, in the case of an editorial layout, some situation or theme.

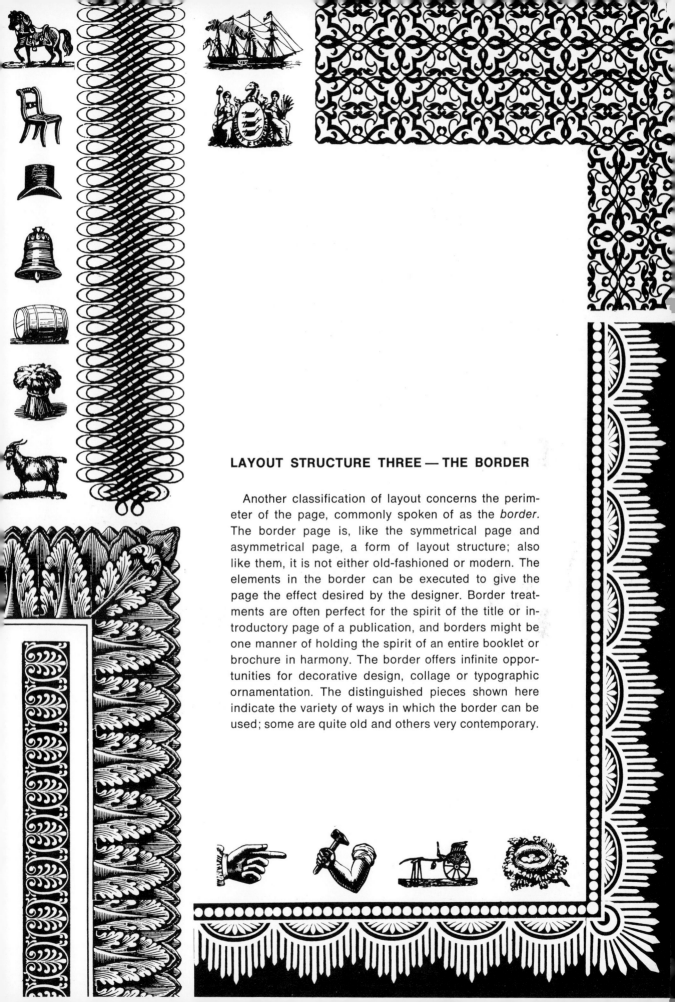

LAYOUT STRUCTURE THREE — THE BORDER

Another classification of layout concerns the perimeter of the page, commonly spoken of as the *border*. The border page is, like the symmetrical page and asymmetrical page, a form of layout structure; also like them, it is not either old-fashioned or modern. The elements in the border can be executed to give the page the effect desired by the designer. Border treatments are often perfect for the spirit of the title or introductory page of a publication, and borders might be one manner of holding the spirit of an entire booklet or brochure in harmony. The border offers infinite opportunities for decorative design, collage or typographic ornamentation. The distinguished pieces shown here indicate the variety of ways in which the border can be used; some are quite old and others very contemporary.

The technique of embossing is so interesting that a special comment is valid here. The elegant example shown above dates from 1837. The original, in the collection of the author, is exquisitely handsome. Embossing is still an available technique and is quite often used in contemporary design, but it is not inexpensive. It involves special embossing plates and printing methods. It is often used where a special effect of quality or elegance is desired, as in invitations, mailing pieces, brochures, and annual reports. When planning to use an embossing it is necessary to confer with the printer for instructions as to procedures.

A
PREVIEW
OF
SPRING

Its colors,
fabrics, wallpapers
and carpets

publication   HOUSE & GARDEN
art director   ALEXANDER LIEBERMAN
art editor   WOLFGANG FYLER
artist   JAY GRESHAM

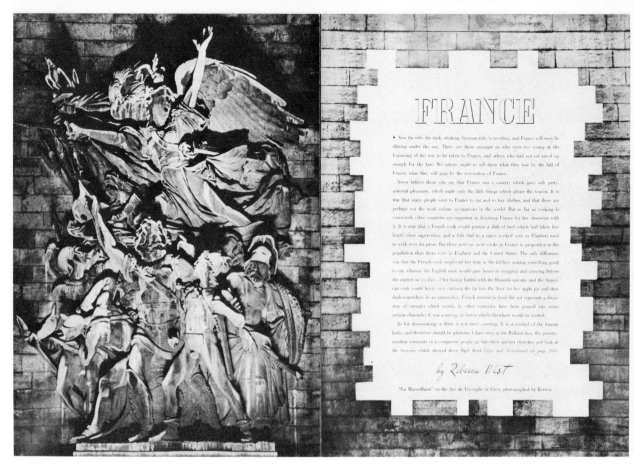

FRANCE

● Now the tide, the dark, stinking, German tide, is receding, and France will soon be
shining under the sun. There are those amongst us who were too young at the
beginning of the war to be taken to France, and others who had not set sail up
enough for the fare. We others ought to tell them what they lost by the fall of
France, what they will gain by the restoration of France.

Never believe those who say that France was a country which gave only petty,
material pleasures, which made only the little things which please the tourist. It is
true that many people went to France to eat and to buy clothes, and that these are
perhaps not the most serious occupations in the world. But so far as cooking is
concerned, other countries are impudent in despising France for her obsession with
it. It is true that a French cook would present a dish of beef which had taken five
hours' close supervision, and a fish clad in a sauce worked over as Flaubert used
to work over his prose. But there were no more cooks in France in proportion to the
population than there were in England and the United States. The only difference
was that the French cook employed her time in the kitchen making something good
to eat, whereas the English cook would pass hours in mopping and rinsing before
she started on another of her losing battles with the Brussels sprouts, and the American cook would hurry over rubbing the fat into the flour for her apple pie and then
dash somewhere in an automobile. French interest in food did not represent a diver-
sion of energies which would, in other countries, have been poured into more
serious channels; it was a saving of forces which elsewhere would be wasted.

As for dressmaking, a dress is not mere covering. It is a symbol of the human
body, and therefore should be glorious. I have seen in the Balkans how the poverty-
stricken remnants of a conquered people go into their ancient churches and look at
the frescoes which showed them their dead kings and *(Continued on page 194)*

by Rebecca West

"La Marseillaise" on the Arc de Triomphe in Paris, photographed by Kertesz

publication   HARPER'S BAZAAR
art director   ALEXEY BRODOVITCH
photographer   KERTESZ

PROJECT ASSIGNMENT: The four illustrations in this section demonstrate com-
pletely different approaches to the border, but they all satisfy the requirements of
design for the border page. Projects in this area almost suggest themselves; approaches are almost limitless in almost any technique. The embossing technique
on page 40 suggests the possibility of preparing a border in some type of semi-
dimension, such as pasted cut-out paper forms or a design applied in modeling
clay, or plaster. Actual objects pasted down, painted or sprayed with flat white
paint and photographed with deep shadows can give exciting effects.

LAYOUT STRUCTURE FOUR — THE GRID

The three forms of layout structure which have been explored thus far — symmetrical, asymmetrical and border — are largely developed through an intuitive sense of design with a minimum of restricting structural organization. A fourth approach to page design, the *grid*, is very carefully structured. It has the virtue of a plotted system of control which, while being useful for a single page or a spread of two pages, can bring a quality of conformity to situations in which several pages are involved. The system divides the pages into planned grids which will accommodate both pictorial and text material. The grids can be planned to be smaller or larger according to the need of the material to be displayed. Resulting pages have a decidedly mechanical appearance, since all elements are rigidly controlled following the basic plan. Shown below is a typical plotting of a double spread in a grid system.

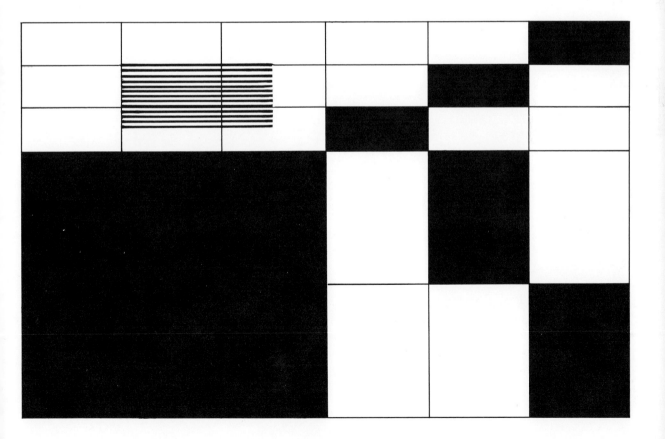

The examples on these pages show applications of the grid principle in actual use. On this page is a double spread, together with a light impression of the spread on which the grid has been indicated.

client CHAMPION PAPERS
publication THE PRINTING SALESMAN'S HERALD, BOOK 20
designer TOMOKO MIHO
photographer RODNEY GALARNEAU
mechanicals KURT KLEIN, INC.

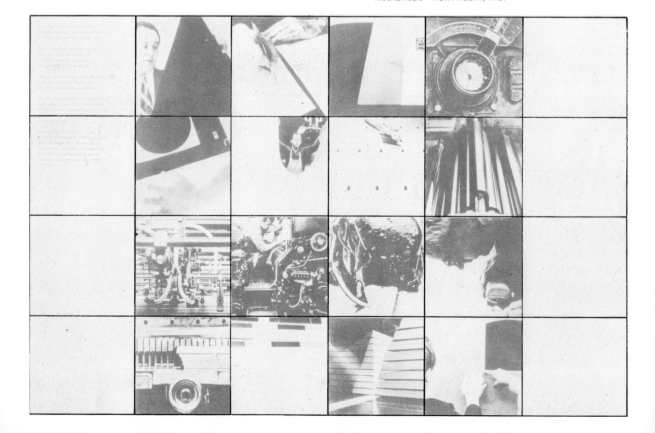

4

FACING UP TO THE NEED Aluminum's versatility has found unparalleled use in commerce, industry and science. In forms and applications that mark our era, aluminum contributes lightness, strength and beauty to an infinite variety of products.

Because its desirable physical and chemical attributes can be augmented with unique finishes, aluminum is often the choice of designers and manufacturers.

To the architect it presents endurance with attractiveness and aesthetic values with utility that persist despite harsh environments.

The designer sees in aluminum an obliging metal that responds to his search for good form and function.

And the consumer's strong attraction to items lightened and beautified with aluminum supports the manufacturer's decision in favor of the metal.

client ALUMINUM COMPANY OF AMERICA
publication THE MANY FACES OF AMERICA
designers GRAPHIC DIRECTIONS, INC.
art director JOHN HOOVER
photographer JOHN HOOVER

PROJECT ASSIGNMENT: Plot a grid page on tracing paper, developing a plan to use photographs, a heading and some text material. Use your best tools for this work — a T-square, angles, etc. — since a grid design should be planned on a very mechanical basis. Plot the page out experimentally in three or four ways and then proceed to develop the design in more complete fashion on Bristol or illustration board. Since grid designs are often planned on the basis of "bleed" pages (see page 78), allow the pictures to go right off the edges of the page if you so desire; you will, of course, have to leave margins around the edges of text material. Pay particular attention to precise vertical and/or horizontal alignments of all material, since this is essential to the spirit of grid designs.

client TV GUIDE MAGAZINE
art director JOHN WILLIAM BROWN
designer WILLIAM KOCH
artist WILLIAM KOCH
photographer GEORGE FARAGHAN

Talk is cheap. Buying isn't. This year, over 2 million of our people will turn words to action. Right on the showroom floor. Maybe yours—if you use our readership leadership to build some action for your words.

UNUSUAL DIMENSIONS IN LAYOUT

In the terminology of the graphic arts the word "layout" suggests the design of a single page, and probably a page with a long vertical dimension. But this is not necessarily the fact. A page may be square, or longer horizontally than vertically; layout may be for double spreads, or even multiple spreads, or a series of pages, or jumbo designs such as are sometimes used in direct mail or for posters. We think most often, too, of a layout as two-dimensional. But the layout artist sometimes becomes involved with items which may almost be called three-dimensional, or at least quasi-three-dimensional. The examples shown on these pages give some idea of extensions of layout to forms that are more than two-dimensional, as do the two interesting designs for calendars on page 48. Layouts for unusual particular situations — such as direct-mail pieces — can be most exciting to work on, since sizes and shapes can often be more varied, and often at the whim of the designer. The designer may also have the opportunity to dictate the kind or color of paper or even the kind of material (acetate, foil, parchment, etc.) on which his project will be printed.

client   CHARLES PFIZER & CO., INC.
agency   WILLIAM DOUGLAS MC ADAMS, INC.
art director VICTOR TRASOFF
artist   JOSEPH LOW

client   THE DRAKE PRESS
art directors JOSEPH GERING, WILLIAM HIRSCH
artist   JOSEPH GERING

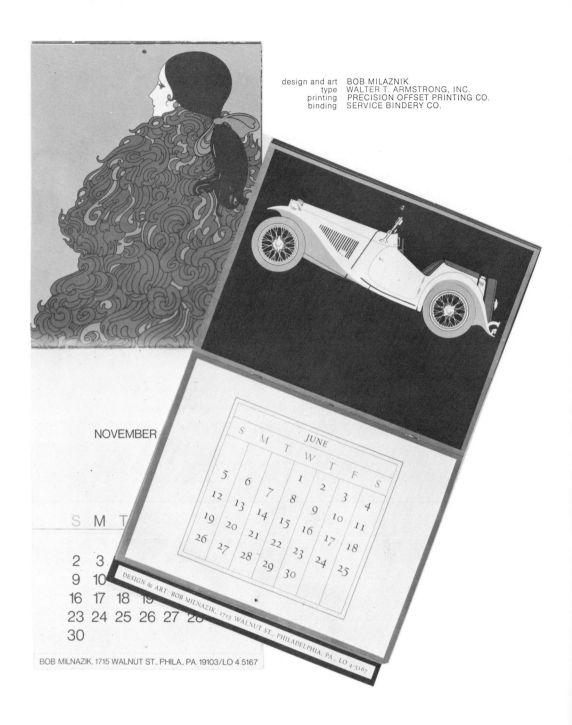

design and art BOB MILAZNIK
type WALTER T. ARMSTRONG, INC.
printing PRECISION OFFSET PRINTING CO.
binding SERVICE BINDERY CO.

PROJECT ASSIGNMENT: This project offers endless opportunity for experiment in the use of paper in different sizes, shapes and foldings. Before making an experiment you should refer to pages 76 and 77. In preparing a folded-dimensional piece it is best to pick an interesting theme to work out — you will note that this has been done on the items on pages 46 and 47, and it was also a feature of the 12 pages of each calendar shown above. For instance, take a subject such as a country. In using features of the country such as flags, scenes, costumes, history and transport you can develop material for the various panels which relate in a most interesting manner. Don't be afraid to use lots of color.

TOOLS AND EQUIPMENT

The next few pages of this book deal with the tools of the layout designer. While the greatest needs of the layout artist are talent, inspiration and imagination, it will soon become evident that an ability to use good tools and equipment is of utmost importance. Good books should head the list of tools. The alert designer should gather a library of books and magazines, not only ones that deal with his profession, but anything that will instruct and stimulate him in his work. These may include books on such subjects as color, design, theater, architecture or travel. Certain books he must have — those on typography, processes of reproduction, paper and papermaking, printing and other subjects related to his function as a layout designer. If you are alert you will be able to add to your library many books and publications on type specimens, paper specimens and demonstrators, printing demonstrators and many, many other subjects. These may be yours for the effort of a telephone call or a letter to a company representative.

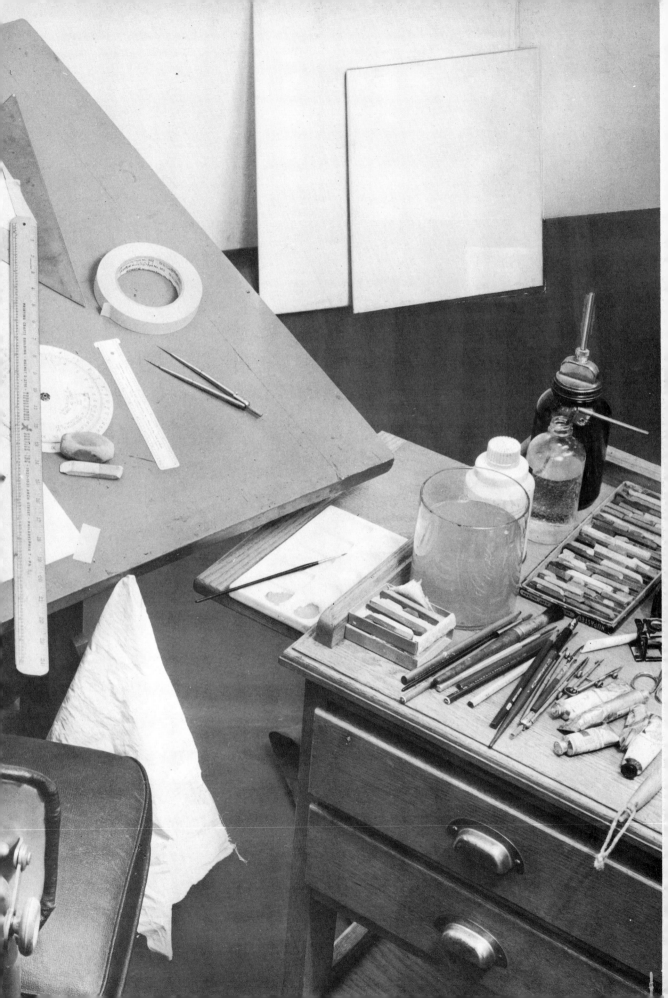

The photograph on the preceding pages shows the simplest kind of equipment. Most of these tools are shown and explained in the pages which follow. Various pencils and brushes of good quality are necessary. The three tools shown at the right, particularly the T-square (steel), should be the best obtainable. (Drop a simple wooden T-square on the floor just once in certain positions and it is out of true and no good!) Not shown on these pages are certain materials, supplies, tools and equipment which the designer will find useful and, often, necessary because of his own growing experiences and needs: for example, a paper-cutting board, a tacking and dry-mount iron, and a camera lucida ("lucy"). The actual outlay for basic equipment for the layout artist is relatively small. Buy only what you will really need, but buy the best quality.

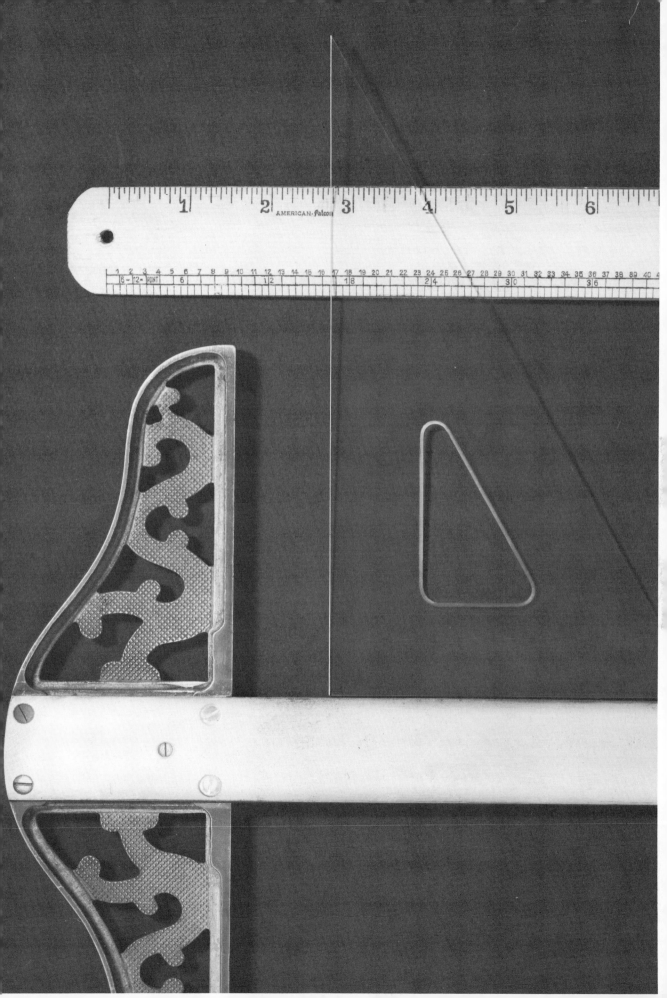

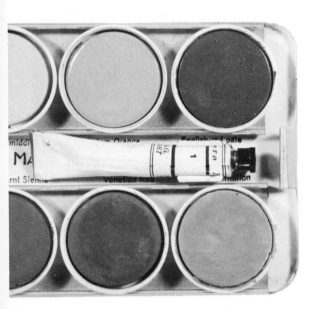

Equipment and supplies for the graphic artist are, of course, manufactured to do specific jobs. For instance, pencils (as shown on page 52) made with lead, carbon, pastel and other materials are planned for particular usages. Lead pencils are marked for degrees of softness or hardness, beginning in the middle with HB (medium) and ranging to 6H (very hard) and to 6B (very soft). Some have flat leads so that they may be sharpened to chisel points, particularly useful in sketch lettering. The new marker-type pencils have gained great popularity. Brushes, too, come in a variety of sizes and styles for specific uses. Small, pointed brushes will be required for very detailed work and for finished lettering, while larger watercolor

brushes will find infinite uses. Large, flat brushes will be needed for laying in large areas of color or poster paints. Pictured on page 54 are a few wet media which are usually applied with a brush. Some, such as watercolor, dyes, and color inks, are intended for use where transparency is desired; others, such as poster, showcard, and retouching paints, are normally used where mat, opaque results are wanted. In addition to pencils, "stick" media include pastels in wide ranges of color and ranges of gray and also lead sticks. A variety of erasers will include kneaded, soap, and ink and pencil types. Penholders and penpoints in profusion will be a part of the designer's kit.

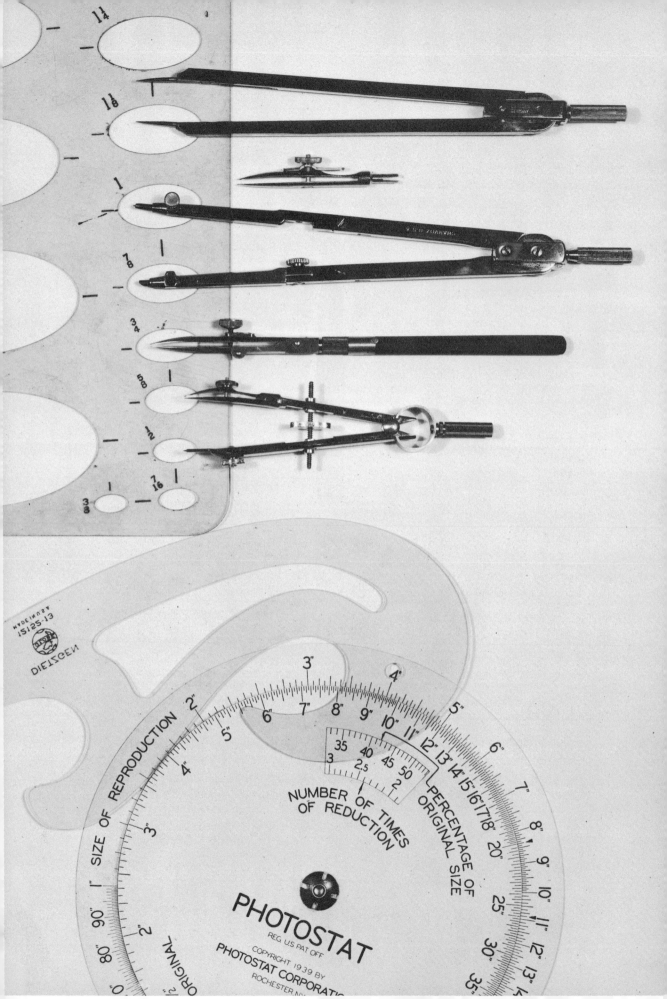

Inevitably the well-equipped studio will have certain tools of a technical nature. These will include: good mechanical-drawing instruments; equipment for drawing ovals and various curves (oval guides and French curves); instruments for ascertaining proportional relationships (one type is shown at the bottom of the opposite page); and a fine airbrush with an air compressor (for, at least, that inevitable whisper of retouching which is often required on both art and photograph). All of these tools are expensive and should be purchased with great selectivity; they deserve to be kept in the best condition. The items pictured below will be most necessary. They include high-grade fixatif, which is used for fixing pencil or chalk work and is applied with an atomizer or from a spray container. Rubber cement is procurable in jars or cans and will be found most convenient to use in the type of dispenser pictured. (A very useful pick-up eraser for the residue of rubber cement can be made by pouring a blob of rubber cement itself on a porcelain palette and allowing it to congeal and dry.) Supplies of tissue, tracing and bond paper pads, Bristol and illustration boards, as well as various types of color papers, will be standard supplies procurable from reliable art-supply stores.

The ability of the Polaroid Land camera to produce what may be termed "instant pictures" is well known. This camera has been found to be an important tool for the graphic designer and is standard equipment in many studios and art departments. There are several models available, together with supplementary equipment which makes them adaptable for many uses. The imaginative designer will find many ways in which these cameras will help him *creatively*; very important is the speed with which they can help visualize creative ideas. The layout to the right is an advertising page prepared by the Polaroid Corporation in collaboration with Doyle Dane Bernbach showing ways in which this distinguished New York advertising agency has found Polaroid Land cameras to be advantageous. In a world in which the creator of design material needs to see his ideas interpreted visually and in which clients want to see them quickly, equipment such as this is vital.

How Doyle Dane Bernbach uses the Polaroid Land camera.

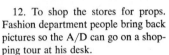
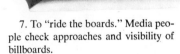

Here are 17 ways.

1. To make original art like this Avis button.

2. To shoot mock-ups. For instance, a model car mounted on a thin round shaft becomes a full-sized automobile on a hydraulic lift.

3. To make a comp. A/D shoots the product. Stats the picture to size. Drops it into the layout. And it's like seeing the finished ad.

4. To make macrophotographs (1, 2 or 3X up of complicated little things like circuits for industrial ads).

5. To find out whether her makeup photographs. Or whether the colors read. And where you need lights and where you need shadows. A Polaroid color print tells you in 60 seconds.

6. To shoot pictures of the sets and costumes in a commercial over to the client for instant (?) approval.

7. To "ride the boards." Media people check approaches and visibility of billboards.

8. To give marketing people a way to check store displays for special promotions and bring back proof of what's up and what's not.

9. To make a test shot (as in the picture below) to see what the lighting will look like.

10. To scout locations for TV and print ads so the A/D, writer, producer, director can pick a place to go without going.

11. To audition models. (Is she photogenic or isn't she? You can tell in a minute.)

12. To shop the stores for props. Fashion department people bring back pictures so the A/D can go on a shopping tour at his desk.

13. To make copy prints of almost anything.

14. To make slides of line work or continuous tone subjects with Polaroid Land Projection Film in roll film equipment. (You can take a shot and project it about four minutes later.)

15. To make instant negatives as well as positives of any subject with Type 55 Positive/Negative 4 x 5 Film in view or press-type cameras.

16. To shoot a storyboard for TV. Prints are exactly the right size for the framing pad.

17. To get a quick idea of how the ad would look by folding the actual Polaroid shot and scribbling type on it.

If you've developed some new ways to use the Polaroid Land camera, please pass them along. We'll thank you. And DDB will, too.

Polaroid Corporation, Cambridge, Massachusetts 02139 Polaroid®

DUTCHESS AND ULSTER COUNTY

FARMERS' ALMANAC,

FOR THE YEAR OF OUR LORD

1871

BEING THE THIRD AFTER BISSEXTILE, OR LEAP YEAR

And (until July 5th) the 95th Year of American Independence.

PUBLISHED BY

JOHN B. FLAGLER,

DEALER IN

BOOKS, STATIONERY, ARTISTS' MATERIALS, MUSIC,

Piano Fortes and Organs,

292 Main Street. : : : POUGHKEEPSIE, N.Y.

JOHN PERRING, **85, STRAND**

PATENT LIGHT HATS
8s 6d & 12s

PERRING'S HATS.

SPURIOUS COMMODITIES are so often foisted on the Public, that they rarely obtain a genuine Article; for no sooner does the industrious artisan display the production of his own ingenuity and labour, than some unprincipled pretender starts up, imitates his goods, copies the purport of his advertisements, and somewhat too obligingly adopts the improvement as his own,—nay, sometimes adopts the *name* by which the sole Inventer had gained his credit and celebrity.

JOHN PERRING, ever grateful for the Patronage he has received for a series of years past, from the **highest circles of Rank and Fashion,** and the Public at large, respectfully announces that he has now on Sale, the largest and

Most Splendid Assortment of HATS in London,

IN 100 DIFFERENT SHAPES,

Suitable for all Classes, from the Peasant to the Peer, and at such Prices as cannot fail to meet the views of the ready-money Purchas er.

SINCE THE INTRODUCTION OF

Hats by Weight, invented in 1827, by Perring,

Numerous cotemporaries have set up in the Neighbourhood, and elsewhere, professing the greatest absurdities as regards the weight and price of Hats, and unless some attention is paid to the address, the purchaser is likely to obtain a mere Copy for an Original; but in order the more effectually to avoid such mistakes, **PERRING** has had manufactured, at a cost of **SIXTY Guineas, a HAT UPON WHEELS,** which may be seen perambulating the Town daily, reminding the observer where **GOOD and CHEAP HATS** may be bought, a Print of which may be seen in the window, at **CECIL HOUSE, 85, STRAND** similar to this bill. The following is a list of Prices, which will not be deviated from:—

Gentlemen's Beaver Hats.

Perring's finest & primest quality, the best that can be made, 3½ ounces weight, or otherwise, in 100 different shapes 21s 0d
Second qualities, ditto 16 0
Perring's newly invented Economic Hats, equal in appearance to the best 12 0
Opera Dress Hats .. .. 12 9 to 18 0
Travelling Hats .. .. .. 8 6 — 12 0

Youths' Hats and Caps.

First Qualities 12 0
Superfine 8 6
Good School Hats 6 6
Best superfine Cloth Caps 6 6
Superfine 4 6

School Caps from .. .. 1 0 to 2 6
Horse-hair Caps in twenty different colours, from 4 6

Gentlemen's Caps.

Summer Caps, for Shooting, Fishing, Travelling, &c. .. .. 5 6 to 8 6
Best Cloth Caps 8 6
Seal & other ditto—Waterproof Caps, various.

Patent Silk Hats.

Good fine 7 6
Ditto best double-edged .. 10 6 to 12 0
Extra light do., 3¾ oz. weight 8 6 — 12 0

Livery Hats.

Beaver, waterproof 12 0
Ditto, best quality 16 0

Silk waterproof 8 6
Best ditto, stout 12 0

Ladies' Riding Hats & Caps.

Hats 3½ ounces weight 12 0
Ditto finest Beaver 21 0
Caps, in Cloth, Horse-hair, &c. 8 6 to 12 0

Summer and Shooting Hats.

Fine Drab 6 6
Ditto Black .. .. .. 8 6 to 10 6
Ditto drab or black, warranted to wear well for twelve months 12 0
Fancy Caps, for Travelling, Smoking, Lounging, &c., combining all the Continental and other Fashions.
Children's Hats and Caps in great variety.

No Connexion whatever with any other House, or with a similar name, there being *only one PERRING,* Inventer of Light Hats, in London, as above.

T. C. Savill, Printer, 107, St. Martin's Lane.

SOME BASICS ABOUT TYPOGRAPHY

On page 18 an exploratory introduction to letters and type forms was presented. We will introduce here some fundamentals about type and type usage which should whet your appetite for deeper study into this fascinating subject. The good layout designer knows a great deal about type and its variety of uses. We cannot devote very much space to the subject in this book, but there are many books available on the history of type and typography, nomenclature, type usage and inspiration; some of these books deserve a place in your graphic arts library. Type manufacturers and typesetters supply literature about their offerings and services, and many of them furnish specimen books and other vital literature free to bona-fide users. The interesting reproduction of the cover of a specimen book on a particular type (below) offered for setting is, in itself, an inspired use of the type forms. A period of work in a type or printing shop or a course in typography are good methods of gaining knowledge about this intriguing craft.

client WALTER T. ARMSTRONG, INC.
art director WALTER T. ARMSTRONG, INC.
designer FRANK SCHROEDER
printer WALTER T. ARMSTRONG, INC.

monotype univers
another first from
WTArmstrong

UNIVERS EXTRA BOLD 75 and 76

The type form shown here is in a category called Old Style or Old Face. These forms are largely characterized by the thicker, slanting serifs (the finishing stroke, or spur, on the stroke of letters) and a general appearance that suggests a pen-drawn letter, from which they developed. The difference between the thin and the thick strokes is often less obvious. Typical Old Style faces are Bembo, Caslon Old Style and Garamond.

The second large category of type is called Modern, although it actually originated before 1800. In these forms there is usually strong contrast between thick and thin strokes and the serifs are usually trim and clean, as in the diagram, right. Unrelated to the pen, these letters were developed by the engraver's tool, and that basic fact is evident. Modern faces include the Bodoni family, Corvinus and Craw Modern.

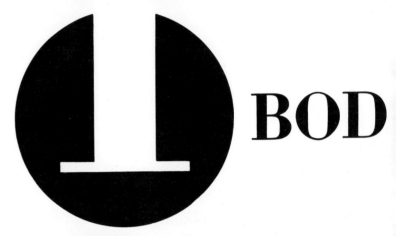

The Contemporary faces include those known as sans-serif (no-serif) forms and the slab-serif or square-serif forms. These have developed as mechanical artist-designed forms and are characterized by little difference between thin and thick strokes in the individual letter. When the thickness of the strokes changes, the terms "light," "medium," "demi-bold," "bold," etc. are used. This group of type faces includes Futura, Stymie, Helvetica and Univers.

The serious page designer has at least a basic knowledge of the history and construction of letters, for this knowledge is essential to the proper use of type forms. The designer should also learn something about the types with which he has to work. Although a universal classification of type faces has never developed, there are divisions which serve to place them in intelligent groupings. The layout artist must understand type sizes (the point system) and the other mechanics and terminologies that are part of the routine of page preparation and production. The charts above will be helpful, but the student should make a deeper study of type with the aid of other books.

The glory and power of Printing is not all in the past. Its influence in the present makes it a powerful conservator of human progress. It is the handmaiden of all the arts and industries, and a most effective worker in the world's workshop, to polish and refine the civilization

ABCDEFGHIJKLM

The glory and power of Printing is not all in the past. Its influence in the present makes it a powerful conservator of human progress. It is the handmaiden of all the arts and industries, and a most effective worker in the world's workshop, to polish and refine the

ABCDEFGHIJKLMN

The glory and power of Printing is not all in the past. Its influence in the present makes it a powerful conservator of human progress. It is the handmaiden of all the arts and industries, and a most effective worker in the world's workshop, to polish and

ABCDEFGHIJKLM

While three classifications of type are basic, a fourth classification is warranted for the enlightenment of the type student. This group includes the Romantic and/or Antique forms, which have had a great revival in recent years. These faces have limited usage but are often used in a manner to recapture the spirit of another era.

BRING BACK OLD-TIMES
SENTIMENTAL

ROUGH VISUALIZATIONS

In the preparation of layouts the designer may, for various reasons, make many preparatory designs in a rough state. Most will be discarded, others will be developed, and some will eventually be carried through to production. The less finished designs prepared are known as roughs (or, sometimes, tissues, since they are mostly done on artist's tissue sketch paper). These roughs may never get any further than the designer's own desk. They may, on the other hand, be used to discuss the approach to the design project with other individuals involved. When an approach has been approved the next design stage may be to prepare a complete comp or dummy of the selected rough. (The word "comp" is related to the words "comprehensive" and "complete.") Comps of a design project are prepared so that a presentation may be made to clients or executives for approval or changes — or sometimes, unhappily, for rejection. These development stages of a layout will be seen on the pages which follow.

Since type in page layout is obviously one of the important elements, there are certain techniques which are fundamental in presenting it even before the time comes to set actual type. In other words, the effect of the type setting must be visualized. On the page to the right the techniques of indicating the appearance of type are demonstrated. On page 66 the copy for setting has been marked with the desired specifications, and on page 67 the type has been set.

It will be noted that indications for large type may be sketched or drawn in to give the effect of the type to be used, whereas smaller type is generally indicated by the two-line method. The distance between the two lines is intended to suggest the size of the *body* of the type to be used, not the size of the ascenders or descenders of the face. If a heavier type is to be suggested the lines are simply made thicker. Specifications to typesetters are often given by notations on the typewritten text, but in many instances the designer may also send along a tissue showing just how he wants the typesetting to look (refer again to page 67).

The glory and power of Printing is not all in the past. Its influence in the present makes it a powerful conservator of human progress. It is the

— CARLYLE.

Cap italic

The glory and power of printing is not all in the past. Its
influence in the present makes it a powerful conservator of
human progress. It is the handmaiden of all the arts and industries, and a most effective worker in the world's workshop,
to polish and refine the civilization of the age.—Carlyle

54

also set Carlon O.S. Italic 47'
36pt. 12pt. leaded + 47 picas
72pt. Cap T 540
set Carlyle O.S. Carlon 18pt. caps

Baskerville 10pt. 3pt. leaded + 20 pi flush L+R

Type and type measurements are not stated in inches but in other units: points, picas, ems, ens, etc. The vertical size of type is stated in points. There are about 72 points to an inch (1 pt. = 0.9962 in.). This might suggest that the letter face of a 12-pt. type would measure 1/6 inch, but it does not. The point size is not the size of the letter form itself, but of the body of metal on which it is formed. Different type families have different characteristics, and these make a confusing difference in the point size as it appears when set; it is difficult to identify the size of a type when seen in print. Below are alphabets of Helvetica, Century Schoolbook and Craw Modern, each in 12-pt. capital letters and in 12-pt. lowercase (small) letters.

ABCDEFGHIJKLMNOPQRSTUVWXYZ
abcdefghijklmnopqrstuvwxyz
ABCDEFGHIJKLMNOPQRSTUVWXYZ
abcdefghijklmnopqrstuvwxyz
ABCDEFGHIJKLMNOPQRSTUVWXYZ
abcdefghijklmnopqrstuvwxyz

The leads (pronounced with a short *e,* like "heads") which are used to add space between lines are also spoken of in point sizes: 1-point, 2-point, etc. The length of a line of type, called its measure, is usually given in picas; 1 pica = 12 pts. A difficult problem for the layout designer is calculating the size of type to fit a given space. The character-count method is universally accepted, although there are other methods in use. To specify type and type sizes one must have specimen sheets or specimen books of available type faces. The illustration above shows a typical piece of typewritten text, and the page at the right shows the setting produced as specified on the typed text. To specify type for a page, first decide the pica width of a column (a pica is about 1/6 inch, but you should own a pica rule) and then decide what type and what size of that type you wish to have set. From the specimen sheet count the number of characters in the width of the line you plan to have set (counting each space between words as one character). Count the same number of characters on your typed text and draw a light pencil line vertically at this place. You will now be able to count the number of full lines needed, and by counting the "overage" you will be able to compute the total number of lines needed. If you desire to set the text in a larger or a smaller size, the character count will, of course, be different.

Note: to fit page requirements the text at the bottom right has been slightly reduced photostatically. It is, therefore, slightly less than the specified 36-pt. size.

THE GLORY AND POWER OF PRINTING is not all in the past. Its influence in the present makes it a powerful conservator of human progress. It is the handmaiden of all the arts and industries, and a most effective worker in the world's workshop, to polish and refine the civilization of the age.—*Carlyle*

T*he glory and power of Printing is not all in the past. Its influence in the present makes it a powerful conservator of human progress. It is the handmaiden of all the arts and industries, and a most effective worker in the world's workshop, to polish and refine the civilization of the age.* — CARLYLE

Dr. Johnson on the art of happiness

THERE IS NOTHING TOO LITTLE

FOR SO LITTLE A CREATURE

AS MAN.  IT IS BY

STUDYING LITTLE THINGS THAT

WE ATTAIN THE GREAT ART

OF HAVING AS LITTLE MISERY

AND AS MUCH HAPPINESS AS

POSSIBLE. (From James Boswell, *The Life of Samuel Johnson, LL.D.,* 1791)

Artist: Arthur Williams

Container Corporation of America

client CONTAINER CORPORATION OF AMERICA
agency N. W. AYER & SON, INC.
art director WALTER REINSEL
artist ARTHUR WILLIAMS

The needs and uses of typography vary tremendously. Some projects require a minimum of type. In others the amount of type and the variety of uses it must be put to are frighteningly complex. Sometimes the most important consideration is only that the type be legible. In other instances special effects are intended, such as in the two pieces reproduced here. In the contemporary design world the variety of available types is incredible, but it is nevertheless the designer's responsibility to specify types that are appropriate from all standpoints — aesthetic, technical and economic.

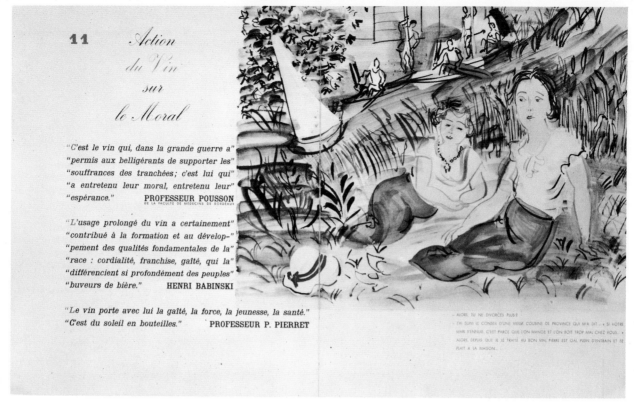

publication MON DOCTEUR LE VIN
publisher DRAEGER FRÈRES
artist RAOUL DUFY
typography A. M. CASSANDRE

PROJECT ASSIGNMENT: First, make some attempt to gather material on type in the form of type specimen sheets or specimen books. Some good books on type are mentioned in the list on page 96. Visits to local printing and typesetting houses may result in handouts of useful material — don't spurn some good used material until you have the opportunity of getting new items. Make some sketches on tissue or tracing paper, in pencil, of some headline type faces from magazines (or your specimen sheets). Trace the letter forms on the tissue placed directly over the types. This is an excellent way to get the feel of different type forms. At the same time see if you can learn the actual names of the types by referring to your type books or specimen sheets. As another project, use the two-line system of indicating lines of type as shown in the example on page 65. Try to give the effect of smaller and larger type faces and of lighter and heavier faces. (Remember that type comes, generally, in sizes from 6-pt. to 72-pt. and that most faces come in *at least* regular and heavy weights — often in other weights as well. Most faces also come in italic forms and some in condensed or extended characters related to the basic forms.) Finally, make some actual layouts on tissue, using photographs or other design or pictorial material, and put in headlines and lay in areas of text material in two-line indications. All in all — learn to know and to *love* type.

Race you to the office.

One test of a city that works is: how easily can you get to it? And back?

To prove our point, we've thrown a ring around Philadelphia–and captured some of the nation's most beautiful suburbs. Beautiful to look at, beautiful to get to and from. (Some of them even *sound* beautiful.)

Catch the express from Paoli in the morning. Thirty honest minutes later, you're in town.

Coming in from the north, you get on at Glenside (25 minutes away) and pass through Jenkintown and Elkins Park.

Moylan, Wallingford, Swarthmore, southwest of the city, are all less than a half hour away.

And the old, established Jersey suburbs to the east are closer than ever because of a new high-speed line.

On the city end of the commute, there's another pleasant surprise. The terminals at which you arrive are just a few minutes' walk from where most people work. Suburban Station is right across the street from Penn Center, one of the country's classic ventures in urban renewal.

If you're thinking about relocating people, a short and pleasant commute from a lovely suburb isn't everything. It's just *one* of the nice things about working in Philadelphia. Interested in some others? Write for your copy of "The Liveable City." Box 000, Philadelphia, Pa. 00000. It was written by someone who lives here.

Philadelphia: The Liveable City

ABOUT PRESENTATIONS

The ultimate objective of the layout designer's activities is to create material which will finally appear as a printed piece, whether it be a page, a spread, a booklet, a brochure or any of a variety of other items. The ultimate objective of the printed piece is to communicate. After the objectives of the piece have been reviewed and after the possible approaches have been considered, a *presentation* to the client, editor, executive or committee will probably be required. The art director and/or the layout designer will be greatly involved in this presentation. This and the five pages following give some insights into presentation procedures. The material shown on these pages was assembled especially for this book from actual material relating to two advertising campaigns prepared by N. W. Ayer & Son, Inc.

Traditionally the usual design activities of the layout artist in preparing printed material may include (1) making his own rough sketches, which may be used in conferring with co-workers in his own organization; (2) preparing more complete roughs or comps, for presentation purposes; (3) procuring or preparing artwork or photography; and (4) preparing the final mechanical art required for printing. Whether the layout artist is responsible for some or all of these activities may depend on the specific situation.

These two pages show examples of a traditional presentation for a double-page advertisement planned to show the advantages of commuting to "Philadelphia: The Liveable City." In this instance it was necessary for the agency to show how the pages would appear to committees of civic groups who might or might not be knowledgeable about the procedures involved. It will be noted that the pictures in the comp at the left are sketches suggesting what the final photographic subject matter will be. It will also be noted that the heading, text and signature for the pages were actually set in type and shown to the client. Text is sometimes "suggested" in presentations rather than going to the expense of setting type before approval. (See page 31.) The finished advertisement as it appeared is shown below. The size of these pages was actually 8⅛″ x 11 3/16″ (thus the double spread was 16¼″ x 11 3/16″). The illustrations were reproduced from full color transparencies.

client ACTION PHILADELPHIA
agency N. W. AYER & SON, INC.
creative director CHUCK MACKEY
art director BILL OLIVER
photographer SHELLY ROSEMAN
copywriters FRANK CUNNINGHAM
ROBERT LASSON

JENKINTOWN
WYNCOTE

11 miles. 21 minutes

MOYLAN-ROSE VALLEY

13 miles. 29 minutes

BERWYN

18 miles. 36 minutes

BRYN MAWR

10 miles. 19 minutes

DEVON

17 miles. 34 minutes

WALLINGFORD

12 miles. 26 minutes

PAOLI

20 miles. 30 minutes

HADDONFIELD

WESTBOUND
PHILADELP

8 miles. 12 minutes

ROSLYN

14 miles. 30 minutes

SWARTHMORE

11 miles. 24 minutes

WAYNE

15 miles. 30 minutes

CHESTNUT HILL

12 miles. 27 minutes

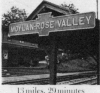

Race you to the office.

One test of a city that works is: how easily can you get to it and back?

To make our point, we've thrown a ring around Philadelphia and captured some of the nation's most beautiful suburbs. Beautiful to look at, beautiful to get to and from. Some of them even sound beautiful.

Catch the express from Paoli in the morning. Thirty honest minutes later, you're in town.

Coming in from the north, you get on at Glenside, 23 minutes away, and pass through Jenkintown and Elkins Park.

Moylan, Wallingford, Swarthmore, southwest of the city, are all less than a half hour away.

And the old, established New Jersey suburbs to the east are closer than ever on the new high-speed line.

On the city end of the commute, there's another pleasant surprise. The terminals are just a few minutes' walk from where most people work. Suburban Station is right across the street from the Penn Center office complex, one of the country's classic ventures in urban renewal.

If you're thinking about relocating people, a short and pleasant commute from a lovely suburb isn't everything. It's just one of the nice things about working in Philadelphia.

Interested in some others? Write to The Liveable City, Box 1227, Philadelphia, Pa. 19105.

Philadelphia: The Liveable City

The presentation procedures in this campaign for the Magazine Publishers Association by N. W. Ayer & Son, Inc., were quite different from the previous example. In this instance a series of advertisements was planned to extol the merits of magazine advertising in relation to other media, and the presentation was made to the executive director of the association. The presentation consisted of ideas presented essentially with a doodle of the proposed pictorial contents of each ad,

Actual size
of original transparencies

Art for Art Smith's sake.

When Kienholz' sculpture, *Back Seat Dodge—'38,* went on display in the Los Angeles Museum, the back door was kept discreetly closed.

But a few months later when it appeared in a national magazine, the door was wide open.

Thirty thousand people saw the sculpture in that museum. In the magazine it was seen just as the artist intended it. And by more than eleven million people.

Magazines, more than anything else, have brought the real world of art into the world of Art Smith's all over the country.

Huge numbers of people will never visit the Sistine Chapel. They may never even visit a museum. Still they can know—and appreciate in color—what art is about. Its history, its meaning and the direction it's moving in now.

And magazines don't back away from touchy subjects in art any more than they do in anything else. They don't have to.

When it comes to stirring up interest and involvement, magazines take a back seat to nobody.

Think about that the next time you want to tell people what you have to sell.

Magazines are the involving medium.
Magazine Publishers Association

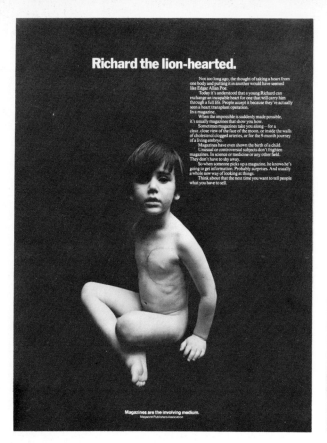

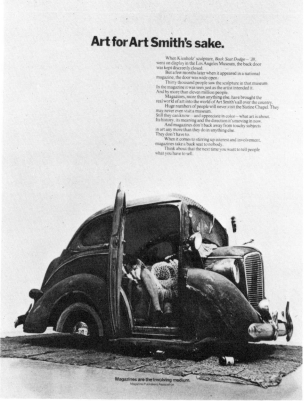

client   MAGAZINE PUBLISHERS ASSOCIATION
agency   N. W. AYER & SON, INC.
creative director   ROBERT DUNNING
art director   ROBERT DUNNING
photographers   JAMES MOORE (fashion)
                CHARLES GOLD (car)
                CARL FISCHER (Richard)
copywriters   DEANNE LEETY
                BLAKE HUNTER

and the barest of typewritten suggestions for the text. These were actually shown to the client and approved, and the task of achieving the intended effect was turned over to creative photographers. It can be seen how well they did their work. It is interesting to note that the photographs for this campaign were taken as 2″ x 2″ or 35mm color transparencies and reproduced in the extremely large page sizes of the campaign — 11³/₈″ x 15¹/₄″. When the transparencies were completed, black-and-white photostatic copies to the full size of the final advertisements were made and the final type for the text material was set. It should be noted that the actual type design for these pages is extremely simple, thus enhancing the quality of the photographs. In addition to clean reproduction proofs of the text, proofs on transparent acetate were also prepared. These proofs were pasted in position on the photostats of each ad, as shown in the illustration on page 73. The dimensions of the finished advertisements were marked on each photostatic dummy, and these, together with the original transparencies and the reproduction proofs of the text, were given to the color engraver. Three of the advertisements for the campaign are shown here; they were all the same size, but the larger reproduction of the one on the right will give some idea of the quality of all. The presentations made to the client appear to be very casual, but it must be understood that the layout artist or art director has to know about all aspects of the work and must be involved in each procedure leading to the final printing.

"But mother...
underwear would hide my fashion accessories."

It wasn't long ago that all exposure was indecent. Today, it's vogue. Admittedly spunky. But not spurned even in the safe suburbs.

How did it happen?

Magazines.

Magazines turned legs into a rainbow. Magazines convinced a gal she needed a flutter of fur where plain, little eyelashes used to wink.

Magazines have the power to make a girl forget her waist exists. And the very next year, make her buy a belt for every dress she owns.

They can move a fashion trend from Paris to the papa-mama store as fast as somebody can sew it up.

Magazines help distressed damsels remake their wardrobes, faces, hair, body. And sometimes their whole way of being.

And the ladies love it. And beg for more.

When she gets involved with herself and fashion, in any magazine, she's a captive cover to cover.

And you can be sure she's looking at everything. Right down to the tiniest ad.

Think about that the next time you want to tell her what you have to sell.

Magazines are the involving medium.
Magazine Publishers Association

PAPER FOLDS

The material on these two pages and the ones following is intended to be suggestive rather than inclusive. When a layout design is prepared for a single page, it is necessary to know the measurements; whether it is to be a margin or bleed page; how many colors are possible; and what reproduction process will be used. When the layout assignment concerns the preparation of several pages, as in a folder or booklet, not only must all this be known, but in addition the foldings must be known or planned by the designer. See the diagram below for a hint of the variations possible. In the case of a booklet, the method of folding the pages must be known and strictly adhered to. Therefore, the strongest advice that can be given here is that the layout designer always check the *mechanics* of his assignment before he so much as lifts his sketching tools. It has been the experience of the author that checking with the printer, production man or any other technical authority may avoid needless — and costly — mistakes and will, in many instances, simplify problems and speed up the preparation of a design. Cooperation between the designer, copywriter, typographer, production man and printer can be essential to the success of the final production.

In the preparation of a printed folder such as any of the forms shown below, the dummy or mock-up of the piece will be made to look as much like the final printed piece as possible. When the folder is approved, however, and the finished art or mechanical is prepared, it must be done in a manner which may be put before the printer's reproduction cameras. Since the piece will, in all probability, print on both sides of the paper, the mechanicals must be laid out in the exact manner in which the material will be printed before it is folded and trimmed. The diagram to the right shows how the material would be positioned on a simple folder such as the one directly below it. A similar planning of the mechanical would be required for any piece shown below. Where and how the material on pages is positioned is called "imposition."

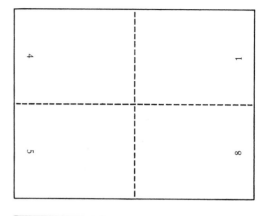

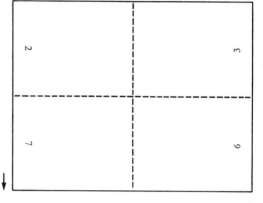

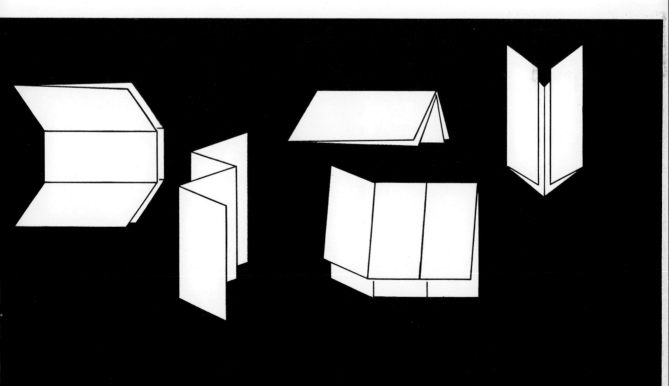

PAGE SIZES

The most important thing to know when beginning a layout is the *size.* Simple as this statement may be, the average student treats this fact quite casually. Since all layouts are prepared to fit somewhere, it is quite necessary to have a knowledge of page sizes, paper folds, page impositions and other details. No designer can be expected to remember all of these things. It is imperative that he at least be aware of them and that he check the mechanical requirements of each assignment thoroughly. The panel below shows some standard areas with which layout designers will be required to work. Magazine page sizes vary, of course, but most of them offer units such as (a) the standard margin page, (b) bleed pages, so called because the design may "bleed" or print off all four edges of the page and is then trimmed, and (c) half-page and quarter-page sizes, which may often vary between vertical or horizontal proportions. Some magazines, as a measure of economy, offer variations such as (d) the "junior" page, half-page and quarter-page sizes, which make it possible to effect economies in plate sizes prepared for other magazines. No dimensions are given on these diagrams because of the obvious variance in magazine page sizes.

a   b

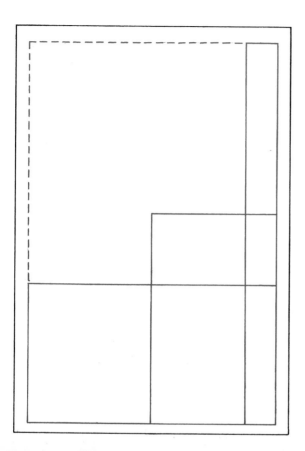

Layout sizes for newspaper advertising are based on a different system, as shown in the diagram to the left. Here the sizes are based on columns and lines, and this terminology has specified meaning. As is well known, newspaper pages are divided into columns, and these columns usually measure about $1\frac{7}{8}$ inches. The depth of these columns is measured in lines — 14 lines to the inch. Thus, a newspaper advertisement 2 columns by 70 lines would be 2 columns wide by 5 inches deep. The same area could be used as 1 column wide by 10 inches deep, or 4 columns by $2\frac{1}{2}$ inches deep.

c

d

PAGE IMPOSITIONS

Pieces of many pages, such as booklets or brochures, are usually prepared on the basis of pages in multiples of 8, 16 or 32 pages. A booklet of, say, 16 pages will be printed on *one* sheet and then folded, bound and cut to make the 16 pages. In this instance, 8 pages will be printed on one side of the sheet and 8 on the other. Two or more colors can be printed on all pages. For reasons of economy

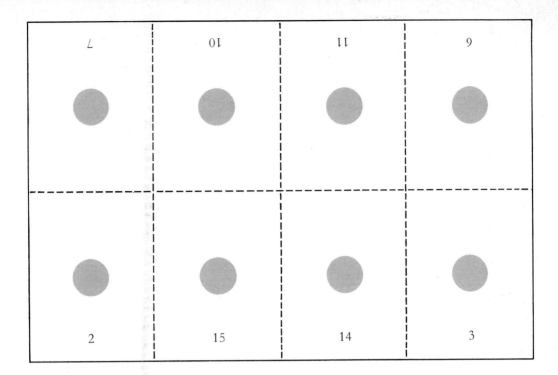

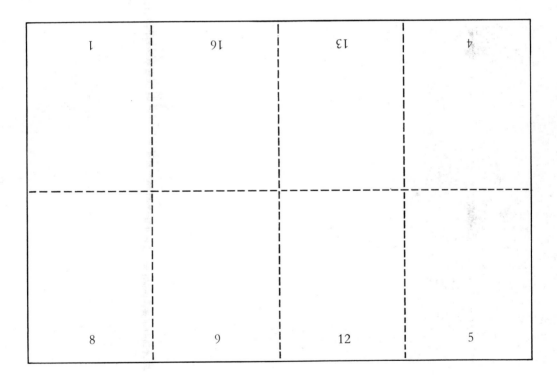

the extra colors are often printed on one side of the sheet only; the position of the colors (imposition) is computed and the mechanicals are prepared accordingly. The diagram above shows a possible imposition of pages to take advantage of a second color on 8 pages of a 16-page form. By experimenting the designer can position a second color to his best advantage. The photograph at left shows how paper can be folded to find the position of the color.

LINE ART AND REPRODUCTION

The methods of reproducing artwork are endlessly fascinating, and the truly creative graphic designer will consider them an important part of his creativity. Artwork prepared in line is the simplest and the least expensive to reproduce. When we speak of "line" we are concerned with artwork that has no tonal values whatsoever — art that is wholly black and white, although it may range from a very thin line to solid areas and even areas of texture. In reproduction, line artwork can be treated in surprising variations, including color.

client   TRIGÉRE
agency   CARL REIMERS COMPANY
art director JAMES DOWNEY
artist   JOSEPH EULA

The handsome fashion illustration reproduced in the ad above was no doubt originally a black line drawing. In the reproduction at the left a screen has been used to create a gray effect. The woodcut below has been reproduced in negative and positive (in color), and the drawing to the right, below, indicates how line art may be prepared to create tonal effects.

client   AMERICAN BAPTIST BD. OF EDUC. AND PUBL.
publication YOUNG PEOPLE, FEBRUARY 6, 1966
art director DAVID MONYER
designer   ROGER HANE
artist   ROGER HANE

$2\frac{1}{8}''$

LINE DRAWING BY EDWARD VALZ

The simple line drawing above, done in black-ink line and without tonal value, makes excellent artwork for line reproduction. All artwork may be done in any size which is comfortable for the best efforts of the artist, but it must be accurately sized in relation to the needs of reproduction. This drawing has been sized in relation to the project on pages 86 and 87. All artwork and photography can be printed by different methods of printing, as diagrammed on pages 90 and 91, but to achieve the printing surfaces (plates) which will print either line or halftone requires photomechanical processes known as *photoengraving.* Simply stated, the preparation of a printing plate involves the making of a negative, the image of which is transferred and etched into the plate. Once the plate is prepared and properly adjusted to the printing press it may be run in any desired color (as well as black) and on an infinite variety of paper surfaces. Although the original art or photograph may have been brilliantly conceived, its total worth has not been achieved until the graphic artist or art director and the printing craftsmen have pooled their knowledge to achieve the best and most interesting results.

While the preparation of a line plate from a line drawing is relatively simple, the making of a halftone plate is more complicated. A halftone plate, below, involves the photographing of continuous-tone artwork or photographs through a glass screen etched with lines. This screen breaks the image into minute dots of varying sizes, which, when reproduced, create an optical effect of tonal variation.

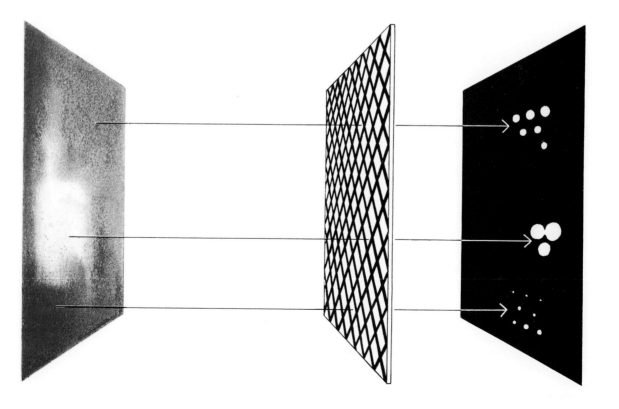

Various methods of reproducing a line drawing: (a) line and mechanical screen; (b) negative line; (c) line in color; (d) two line plates; and (e) negative line in color. To the right, preparation of artwork for a two-color folder. These drawings are known as mechanicals or separations.

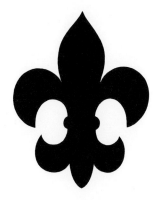

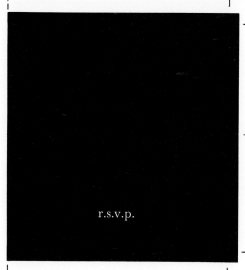

r.s.v.p.

The artwork for the color plate is shown at left and includes the extra $\frac{1}{8}$ inch needed for the bleed.

A negative photostat of type has been pasted in position. Crop and fold marks have been drawn in and register marks are in position.

You are cordially invited to

the opening and reception

THE FLEUR-DE-LIS ROOM

Friday afternoon, April 24th

four to six

This drawing and the type setting are for the black plate and will be positioned with the artwork for the second color as shown in the reproduction below.

The finished invitation is shown below as it will appear when printed with two line plates in two colors.

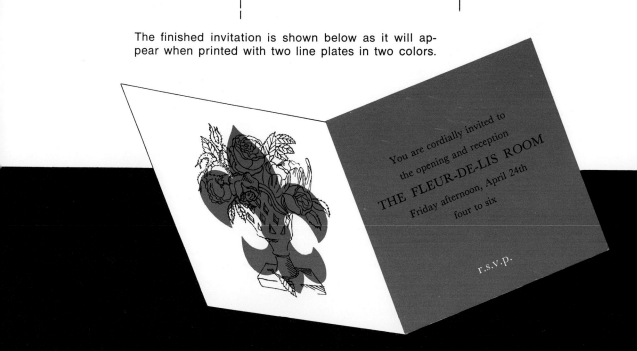

HALFTONE ART AND REPRODUCTION

When subjects to be reproduced are in continuous gray tones (instead of line) as in this handsome photograph of white objects, they must be converted into what are known as halftones. Both halftone and line plates may be prepared for the major methods of printing as shown on the following pages, and they may bleed to the edge (like this page), be scaled to specific sizes or proportions, be silhouetted (as the French houses opposite), etc. Halftone plates, like line plates, may be printed in any color ink desired, and they are used in many ways as is suggested in the pages which follow.

PHOTOGRAPH BY DAN MOERDER

The examples shown here are mostly photographic, but wash drawings and other forms of art may be reproduced by halftone. Note that the face of the Indian has actually been designed with the use of a print of enlarged halftone screen. The linen counter (right) is a handy tool for studying the enlargement of screens and for other studio uses.

client   R. R. DONNELLEY & SONS COMPANY
art director   WALTER L. HOWE
artist   MORTON GOLDSHOLL

here and there at Donnelley's

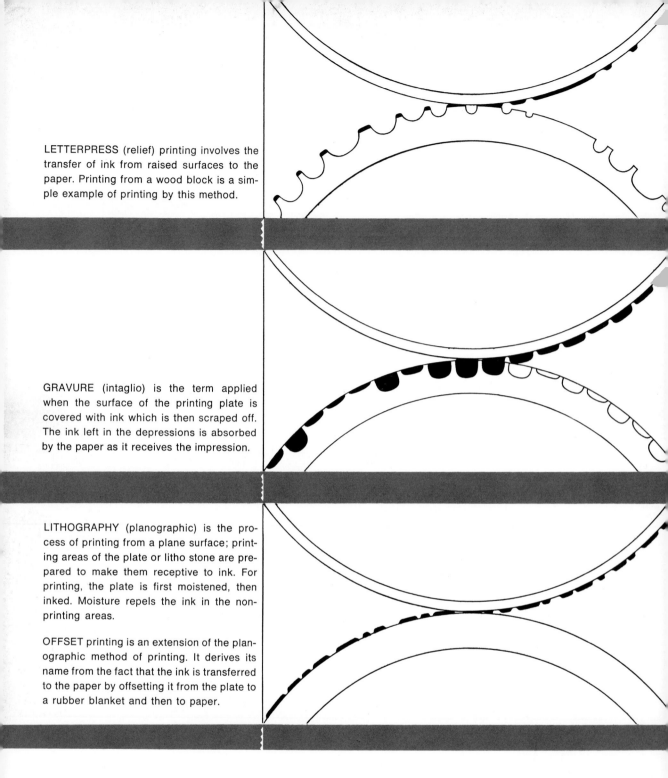

LETTERPRESS (relief) printing involves the transfer of ink from raised surfaces to the paper. Printing from a wood block is a simple example of printing by this method.

GRAVURE (intaglio) is the term applied when the surface of the printing plate is covered with ink which is then scraped off. The ink left in the depressions is absorbed by the paper as it receives the impression.

LITHOGRAPHY (planographic) is the process of printing from a plane surface; printing areas of the plate or litho stone are prepared to make them receptive to ink. For printing, the plate is first moistened, then inked. Moisture repels the ink in the non-printing areas.

OFFSET printing is an extension of the planographic method of printing. It derives its name from the fact that the ink is transferred to the paper by offsetting it from the plate to a rubber blanket and then to paper.

The three basic methods of printing are diagrammed in the columns above. While confusing trade names are sometimes applied to one method or another, essentially the methods are spoken of as letterpress, gravure and offset.

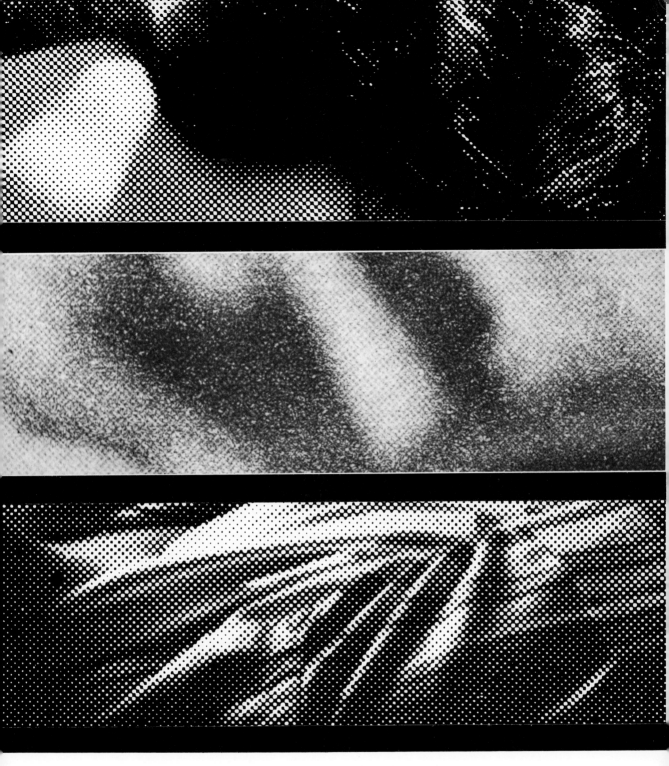

The enlargements, above, show the character of the screen in printing from, respectively, letterpress, gravure and offset processes. The choice of which process to use may often be decided by the layout artist, for his experience will teach him the virtues and limitations of each process in relation to specific situations. Other factors, such as cost requirements, paper, or speed and quantity of production, may come into these decisions, as well as the processes available from specific printers.

When preparing a subject for halftone reproduction a designer can specify a certain screen that he considers appropriate to the purpose of the reproduction. A faithful and subtle reproduction of a photograph can be made, for instance, by the printer's use of a 133-line screen in the preparation of a printing plate, as seen in the first panel to the left above (see diagram bottom of page 85). For printing on coarse newspaper print, a 65-line screen might be used, as in center above. For other special purposes or effects the designer may care to experiment with standard printing screens to which he may add dots, lines or other patterns added by overlay acetates which are available for such purposes.

Good designers take advantage of the possibility of preparing original art or photographs for specific effects. The three reproductions on this page show how the negative of a photograph can be manipulated for particular purposes; the reproductions here and on the preceding page were all made from the same negative. The print for the reproduction at the top left was prepared on a normal photographic paper. The print at the top right was prepared on a hard, contrasty paper, and the one at the right was processed so that a line reproduction could be used.

The reproductions here show further extensions in the treatment of halftone plates involving the use of color and of two printings. As has been previously stated, any halftone plate can be printed in any color of ink specified, as shown at the top left. The reproduction at the top right shows a very common usage of a halftone printed in black over a solid color. The reproduction at the left demonstrates printing in duotone, in which two halftones have been used — one printed in black and the other in color. Duotones, and also three-color printings, are often used to achieve a certain effect of color without the high cost of four-color printing.